What Reviewers Are Say...
Hot Flashes from Hea...

"I experienced a hot flash from laughing so hard while reading *Hot Flashes from Heaven* and then a power surge from all the wonderful, practical advice."

DEBBIE MACOMBER, NUMBER ONE
NEW YORK TIMES BESTSELLING AUTHOR

"I applaud Ronna Snyder for being real about menopause's ups and downs in *Hot Flashes from Heaven*. This girlfriend 'tells it like it is,' but she doesn't leave us in a sweat. Instead, she shows firsthand how God can *use* The Change to change our relationships, goals, and very sense of self when we listen for *His* voice in the hormonal storm."

JANE JOHNSON STRUCK, EDITOR,
TODAY'S CHRISTIAN WOMAN MAGAZINE

"Ronna will take you on a wild ride through her midlife experience that women of all ages and backgrounds can appreciate. *Hot Flashes from Heaven* is a journey through menopause and a reality check that you CAN and WILL come out of your midlife crisis wiser, stronger...and HOTTER!"

MICHELLE JAHNKE, ASSOCIATE PRODUCER,
LIFE FOCUS PRODUCTIONS, THE TBN CHANNEL

"Ronna's candid yet colorful style of writing puts a witty exclamation point on the subject of menopause. Part handbook, part memoir, *Hot Flashes from Heaven* is a must read for any woman heading into that great change of life and aching to find a deeper meaning to it all."

GENEVIEVE SCHMITT, MOTORCYCLE INDUSTRY AUTHORITY
ON WOMEN AND MOTORCYCLING; FOUNDER, WOMENRIDERSNOW.COM

Hot Flashes from Heaven

Ronna Snyder

HARVEST HOUSE PUBLISHERS

EUGENE, OREGON

Cover by Garborg Design Works, Savage, Minnesota

Cover illustration © Garborg Design Works

Published in association with the Books & Such Literary Agency, 52 Mission Circle, Suite 122, PMB 170, Santa Rosa, CA 95409-5370

Names and details of stories have been changed to provide people with privacy.

Every effort has been made to give proper credit for all stories, poems, and quotations. If for any reason proper credit has not been given, please notify the author or publisher and proper notation will be given on future printing.

HOT FLASHES FROM HEAVEN
Copyright © 2008 by Ronna Snyder
Published by Harvest House Publishers
Eugene, Oregon 97402
www.harvesthousepublishers.com

Library of Congress Cataloging-in-Publication Data
   Snyder, Ronna, 1951-
   Hot flashes from heaven / Ronna Snyder.
     p. cm.
   ISBN-13: 978-0-7369-2031-5
   ISBN-10: 0-7369-2031-5
   1. Middle-aged women—Religious life. 2. Menopause—Religious aspects—Christianity.
   3. Middle-aged women—Health and hygiene. I. Title.
   BV4579.5.S69 2007
   248.8'43—dc22

                        2007019261

Printed in the United States of America

08 09 10 11 12 13 14 15 16 / BP-SK / 11 10 9 8 7 6 5 4 3 2 1

Dedications & Acknowledgments

THANK YOU...

To my husband, Bill, who has continued to love me through every single Hot Flash, whether it felt like it was coming from heaven or, uh, that other place.

To all my children and their mates, who have always made me feel that, even at this advanced age, I still just might think, talk, act, and look a smidge "hot"— even when I'm not.

To my mother, whose zealous love for both her family and a well-written book, has led me to lean on the former as I try to write the latter.

To Juli Thorson, the "nag-mag queen," who editorially mentored me until I could leave the "round pen" and lope on my own "ink."

To Niki Anderson, bestselling-author confidant; Margueriette Travaille; and Theresa Schinzel; three dear friends who never fail to bring out the best in me—and in my writing.

To Mark Cornelius, probably the only counselor in the world who could build up a broken-down, middle-aged broad enough to allow her to think she really CAN ride an outrageously purple Harley-Davidson right into a more empowered life.

To Anne Lamott, bestselling author, who's been described as a fellow cranky Christian; and to Max Lucado, who is anything but. Your ever-real and contrastingly different writing styles have inspired me beyond words—cranky or not.

To Terry Glaspey and Carolyn McCready at Harvest House Publishers, who dared to look beyond this also cranky Christian to the heart within and gave me the courage to write "right to the edge," promising that they'd catch me if I went over it. I'm holding you to that promise.

To my agent, Janet Grant of Books & Such Literary Agency, who won my heart when, after years of writing magazine articles to an editor's voice, she dared me to "fight for your own voice." I am woman; hear me roar, girlfriend.

To Costco and Wal-Mart, where I've had some of my most profound Hot Flashes from Heaven. Who'd a thunk it? PS: I don't want a single refund for any of them!

A Word About "Power Surges"

A common menopausal saying goes something like this: "I'm not having a hot flash. I'm having a *power surge!*" Therefore, at the beginning of each chapter, you'll find Hot Flash-filled power surges in the form of quotes that form the foundations for principles outlined in the chapter. Savor them the way you would a good hit of estrogen. You can't overdose on this stuff!

○ ○ ○ ○ ○

A Word About "Mental-Pauses"

At the end of each chapter of *Hot Flashes from Heaven,* you'll find another estrogen-laden treat—a "Mental-Pause." This is the term I've adopted to identify additional tools, facts, actions, or thoughts that have helped me to further ponder the little life lessons Hot Flashes from Heaven have taught me. Perhaps you'll view them as I have: As high-impact, emotionally aerobic mental exercises to expand, educate, and enrich midlife perspectives. "Pause" to reflect upon them or use them as a springboard for discussion in your book club, menopausal support group, Bible study, Red Hat Society, or Blue Thong meetings (yes, there really are such things!). Like real-life stretch marks earned so many years ago, these insights and internal questions and answers, and the actions they have sometimes prompted, have left an indelible mark on who I am and who I'm "changing" into. May they do the same for you.

Contents

Although the Lord gives you the bread of adversity and the water of affliction [in midlife], your teachers will be hidden no more; with your own eyes you will see them. Whether you turn to the right or to the left, your ears will hear [Hot Flashes from Heaven] within you, saying, "This is the way; walk in it."

ISAIAH 30:20-21

(PARAPHRASED, WITH ALL DUE RESPECT
TO MY FRIEND, GOD, BY RONNA SNYDER.)

1

Say What?
Menopause?

You've got to be kidding!
Isn't that for old people?

You are as young as your faith, as old as your doubt;
as young as your self-confidence, as old as your fear;
as young as your hope, as old as your despair.

DOUGLAS MACARTHUR

Then the LORD said, "I will surely return to you about this
time next year, and Sarah your wife will have a son." Now
Sarah was listening at the entrance to the tent, which was
behind him. Abraham and Sarah were already old and well
advanced in years, and Sarah was past the age of childbearing.
So Sarah laughed to herself as she thought, "After I am worn
out and my master is old, will I now have this pleasure?"

GENESIS 18:10-12

The teacup shook in my 44-year-old fingers so precariously that the nurse pouring the herbal brew asked me to hold it with both hands lest it wind up in my lap. I'm sure it was chamomile something or other. I was, after all, in the office of a holistic family practice doctor well known for his outside the box approach to modern medicine. More than one of his patients had referred me to him after I'd explained to them how out of sorts I'd been feeling in both my body and my brain. Chamomile aside, that day I would have much preferred an IV of straight vodka.

He looked at me kindly over his reading glasses. Soft music played dreamily in the background over the soothing trickle of his in-office water fountain. If it was supposed to calm me, it went in one ear and out the other.

"I know you've come to me for natural alternatives for whatever is troubling you," he said as his eyes scanned my chart filled with a litany of physical and psychological symptoms from tingling muscle tension and insomnia to a chronic feeling of depressionlike sadness, worry, anxiety, and unrest. "But frankly, Ronna," he said, glancing not so discreetly at my trembling hands, "you need more."

Translation in my mind? "You're a mess, Mama. Not an herb in the world is tough enough to handle what I'm seeing in your body language and hearing in your voice. We're goin' for the big guns, baby. We're goin' for drugs."

He began scribbling out a prescription just as had all the other doctors I'd seen. And, just as with all the other doctors—male and female alike—I walked out of his office without a definitive diagnosis. Man, I was getting tired of this.

○ ○ ○ ○ ○

I have been where you are, dear sister—thumbing through books looking for answers to midlife questions I didn't even know how to ask.

I have been so deep in the hormonally charged midlife "bread of adversity and water of affliction" (so succinctly described in Isaiah 30:20), that it felt as though I couldn't hear or see my way out of them.

Perhaps as you are doing right now, I ducked low and hid behind the health and self-improvement section of my local bookstore. Despite my linguistic adeptness (as a freelance writer I get paid by the word), I simply hadn't been able to come up with the right ones to explain to those many doctors just how strange my body and my brain were feeling these days.

Like that holistic doc in those early years, they'd run their tests on me, throw out a lot of vague, scary, confusing terms such as fibromyalgia, chronic fatigue, multiple sclerosis, and even rheumatoid arthritis; and then, unable to come up with a definitive diagnosis, pass me off to yet another specialist.

The last one I saw, a while after that visit to the holistic guy, was the top dog in his field—or so I was told by the numerous physicians who recommended him to me. Dr. Top Dog went through my records as though he were looking for a proverbial, needle-sized bone of a diagnosis in a haystack of bad health.

"I have no idea what your problem is, Ronna," he finally said to me that day in his office. "But my sister feels the same way, and I don't know what to do to help her, either." I left more bewildered than when I'd walked into his office.

Then I headed for that bookstore where I'd hoped I'd find a flicker of a clue to what my problem was on some of its pages. I perused a book on depression and promptly burst into tears. Too ashamed and, ironically, too depressed to buy the book, I hustled out of the store before the clerk could see my puffy red face and tearstained cheeks.

"What is wrong with me, God?" I cried out, my hands on the steering wheel of my car. I was sobbing too loudly to hear a reply.

With my automobile still in park, I turned on my local Christian rock radio station, hoping that the upbeat music it usually plays would somehow sooth my jangled nerves. Instead I heard a gentle but authoritative female voice listing off a veritable plethora of mental and physical symptoms. I was in shock as I heard her rattle off words like "internal shakiness, aching muscles and joints, racing heartbeat, inability to sleep, uneasiness, and inescapable sadness." I couldn't believe my ears. She was describing me!

I turned the radio up louder and listened expectantly for her diagnosis. I forgot everything else she said as I heard the one word I'd never even considered: "Menopause."

Say what? Menopause? Isn't that for *old* people frozen in some geriatric ice age?

Like when you're 80 or 90?

I was still just a kid in my forties, but could *that* be what these seemingly random symptoms were all about? Could that be what was messing with my health, but even more important, with my head? The "horror-monal" hailstorm called *menopause?* The dreaded *"Big M"?*

I processed that "M" word over and over in my brain, and then I heard the gentle words that would begin to tranquilize my troubled soul: *"You're entering menopause, Daughter, and this will be a* good *thing."*

The echoing aftereffects of those words felt like a nuclear-charged mental mushroom cloud of understanding and peace throughout my entire, tormented being. I wasn't crazy? I wasn't dying? I was simply... what was the word I was searching for? I was...*changing?*

Yes, I was joining the dubiously elite group of 6000 American women a day who are now entering "The Change of Life." And that transformation, I'd soon learn, was as much about things mental as medical.

That was my first taste of what I've now permanently come to call "Hot Flashes from Heaven," lightning bolts of God-breathed insights intended just for me—and girlfriends like you—at this particularly confusing time in life. As the years unfolded, I'd find out that there would be many, many more.

And they would serve me well. They would elucidate dark and scary issues with clarity and calmness; spirit and strength; purpose and peace; and, yes, sometimes even pleasure. The kind of pleasure the Bible's aging Sarah actually mocked when she first heard that God intended to do great things with her life in her final years.

Lord, don't let us be so foolish.

These hormonally challenged revelations would form a bedrock of stability in my life when nothing else seemed stable. And they would be a perpetual reminder that even if my hormones—and sometimes my sanity—had left me, God had not.

My tears dried almost instantly as I recognized the truth this first internal earthquake of Hot Flashes from Heaven had illuminated.

"Of course! Menopause! Why hadn't *I* thought of *that?*" I asked myself as I felt the beginnings of a smile crease my tearstained cheeks. It was as though the Red Sea had just opened up and let me view the midlife ground I was now walking on. *How did I get here?* I wondered to myself. I thought I was young. And now, well, maybe I'm not.

In my search for answers, I must admit, I'd failed to do the obvious: Consult a gynecologist. My problems, after all, hadn't seemed gynecological. True, my periods were a little whacky once in a while, and so was I. Nevertheless, there had been so many baffling symptoms—like the muscle tension that had left me shaking so badly I couldn't hold that teacup without spilling it. Or the worrisome insomnia and anxiety that had left both my heart and my mind racing so fast it had taken an EKG machine to track them.

Mixed in with all the physical stuff had been that sinking mindset I just couldn't shake. A type of uneasiness whose roots I somehow couldn't unearth. The vague, unsettled feeling that I was being swept up in something much larger than myself. The same feeling I'd had when I'd started my first period, conceived my first child, birthed my first baby. But those were, for the most part, positive feelings. This felt so negative that I'd never connected the physical and psychological dots and concluded that I needed to see a gynecologist.

And not one doctor, male or female, over the months and months of seeing them, had suggested I see one either. Nor had any of them mentioned that this one little word I was hearing on the radio—and the enormous stage of life it has come to represent in our culture—just might be responsible for many of the things I was experiencing. I jammed my car into gear and sped to another bookstore (I was too embarrassed to reenter the first one) where I hoped to find more answers.

I learned that, in one way or another, virtually all the myriad physical and psychological symptoms I'd been complaining about were on a list of menopausal indicators (see the Mental-Pause at the end of this chapter). I also learned that this time that's so aptly called "The Change" begins long *before* menses stop in a hormonal, emotional, and sometimes-spiritual time-warp called perimenopause (premenopause). The books said that oftentimes this precursor stage creeps up on a woman six months to ten years *before* "The Big M," with the average age of the onset of perimenopause at age 41 and menopause—the complete cessation of periods—at 51.

I learned about natural alternatives to synthetic hormones—such as yam-based lotions, flaxseed, soy, and black cohosh for hot flashes; valerian teas for anxiety—and I started taking some of them. I discovered I could actually control a good portion of what was physically bothering me by getting a whole lot more rest than I had needed in my younger, more resilient years. So I pummeled my pride and obtained some much-needed pharmaceutical help to battle my sanity-sucking insomnia and down-in-the-dumps feelings (symptoms listed on the meno-list in the following Mental-Pause).

But there were a lot of things about this unusual time in life that I couldn't learn from books in the bookstore. And, frankly, that's why this one has been written. Despite our enlightened age, there just aren't many tomes out there that offer "girl-speak for the estrogen challenged"; books that delve into the stew pot of emotions and issues we women, who are either entering or adapting to midlife, sometimes feel we're drowning in. I'll say it again: Menopause really, truly, is as much about the brain as it is the body. And so this book, for the most part, is about those menopausal mental and midlife changes you would largely discuss with your girlfriends—not your gynecologist.

You see, it ain't called "The Change" for nuttin', honey.

And it's most certainly not "*just* a hormone thang," either.

I've discovered that, if we look hard enough for them, God has filled this time of dramatic transition in a woman's life with explosively blessed Hot Flashes from Heaven. *All* of us midlifers who have the dominant X chromosome experience these hormonally fueled "ah-haaaa" moments.

But most of us are too busy, stressed, or *dis*tressed to stop and listen to them as they unfold in our minds, bodies, souls, psyches, and lives. Most of us are swept up in the turbulence of aging and miss these powerful vignettes in life that seem sent directly from the heavens to teach us the sacred lessons only mature womanhood has to offer: Instruction and insights about where we've been on life's road. And where we're going.

I've found that these snippets of midlife-related revelations are found—like the sweet and simple voice of God—in our everyday lives. And if we heed them, they can make all of life—even "The Pause"—an amazing learning experience and growing older not nearly so ominous. The fact that these insights are turbocharged by changing hormones that make us more sensitive and seeking is *not* a bad thing. It's what catapults our minds, bodies, souls, psyches, and lives into *true* change.

But I had to learn to listen for these Hot Flashes from Heaven. Otherwise the raw emotions of this season would have been far too much for my feminine heart to bear.

As I've received them and allowed them to put meaning into my own life, I've randomly filled the body of this book. And I've pondered them regularly the way I hope you (and perhaps even your loved ones who are struggling to understand you) will do. As I have, I've discovered that there is a depth and richness to this time that I wouldn't trade for all the quick minds and un-sagging, perky young body parts in the world. That's saying a lot for me—a woman who began adulthood, in part, as a professional television model and radio station marketing manager whose mind and body needed to be in tip-top form.

I've now come to realize that God has given us middle-aged women this time in our lives as a very special gift.

The Change definitely is a time for all that its name invokes. A time to finally let go of the fantasy that we ever had all the answers on how to "do" life properly. A time to ditch youthful misconceptions that if we just did everything correctly, life would turn out all right. A time to consider topics we may have dodged all our lifetime: Is eternal life real? Is anyone *really* up there (as we roll our eyes annoyingly to the heavens) who cares about what's going on down here? Is anyone *really* in charge of this mess called life?

For those of us who opt to believe that more is waiting for us at the end of this life, then midlife becomes the perfect time to stare down wrinkled expectations, aging dreams and bodies, and even death as we learn to more fully embrace a Holy Husband, a Providential Provider. Yup, I mean God—the "Creator of Our Hormones or Lack Thereof." A time to, if we haven't already, fully trust that faithful God-Guy who doesn't give a rip if the stretch marks on our bellies or the varicose veins on our legs look like a Rand McNally map; who really only cares if our minds and hearts are open enough to hear His voice resounding in our life like Hot Flashes from Heaven.

For the rest of us doubting Thomases, this time in life is often the last precursor to making final decisions about questions we've long forgotten to answer or even ask ourselves; the one that often haunted us in our teen years when, ironically, hormonal changes were also fueling internal introspections with questions such as: Who am I *really*? What am I here for? What do I want to do with the rest of my life? Is there someone bigger than life itself—anywhere—who just might love and care about *me*?

If you get even one truth from this book, let it be that menopause, and the midlife juncture it arrives in, is truly *not* a curse.

I've personally found that it is a change point ignited by evolving hormones that lead us into an equally precious, equally ordained time to reflect. A time to remember. A time to reinvent. A time to reevaluate. A time to reconfigure. A time to remind me—and a time to remind you—that the mercies of the heavens, and their abundant life lessons, really *are* new *every*day. Even as we grow ever older. Maybe even especially as we grow ever older. Hot flashing or not.

May the following true stories be all of that and more for you.

●●●●●●●● **MENTAL-PAUSE:** ●●●●●●●

Don't Expect Any Guy to Fully Get It

After receiving my first Hot Flash from Heaven via my car's radio that day, I returned to the doctor who had said his sister had the same symptoms and mental conditions as I.

"How old is your sister?" I asked him, almost certain of his answer.

"Fifty-one," was his reply.

"Did you ever consider that the stuff she's going through just might be menopause related?" I handed him a list of the following symptoms of perimenopause and menopause.

Even though I promised you that this book is more about what our brains go through during The Big M than what our bodies do, it doesn't hurt to know the physical markers that often herald the arrival of The Change of Life. Consider the following as a simple self-test to discover if you, too, are entering into it.

(If you've recently had a hysterectomy or are in your late-thirties and check more than three symptoms that are troublesome to you, you might consider seeing a gynecologist and discussing perimenopausal possibilities. If you're older than that, definitely seek out an evaluation by a doctor or nurse practitioner who specializes in the treatment of menopause.)

- ☐ hot flashes (or periods of warmth or chills)
- ☐ mood swings (from elated highs to introspective, weepy lows)
- ☐ insomnia
- ☐ depression
- ☐ anxiety
- ☐ fatigue (sometimes extreme)
- ☐ irritability

- ☐ night sweats
- ☐ vaginal dryness, odor, or atrophy
- ☐ hair growth on face
- ☐ painful sex
- ☐ loss of sexual desire
- ☐ urinary tract infections
- ☐ weird dreams
- ☐ lower back pain
- ☐ itching of the vulva
- ☐ bloatedness
- ☐ flatulence
- ☐ indigestion
- ☐ osteoporosis
- ☐ aching ankles, knees, wrists, shoulders
- ☐ sore heels
- ☐ thinning scalp
- ☐ frequent urination
- ☐ snoring
- ☐ sore breasts
- ☐ palpitations
- ☐ urinary leakage
- ☐ swollen veins
- ☐ dizzy spells
- ☐ vertigo
- ☐ panic attacks
- ☐ migraine headaches
- ☐ skin feeling crawly
- ☐ memory lapses (brain fog)

Now back to my final meeting with my doctor friend. You could have heard the doc's heartbeat sans stethoscope in the stunned silence that filled the room as he looked, slack jawed, at each one of the above symptoms on the list.

"Uhhhhh, no, I'd never considered menopause," he finally answered. "But you can be darn sure I will."

Men, no matter how well-meaning, will never completely get it when it comes to understanding this unique time in a woman's life, mind, body, psyche, and soul. But that's okay. The Great Physician in the Sky is more than able to make up for it as He sends each one of us women prescriptions for life. Our own personal Hot Flashes from Heaven to light up this sometimes darkly lit pathway so aptly coined The Change of Life.

2

It Ain't Called "The Change" for Nothin', Honey

Embracing "The Change."
Yeah, right.

● ● ● ● ● ● ● ● **POWER SURGES** ● ● ● ● ● ● ● ●

Purple is the most empowering color there is.
People who pick this color are consciously or subconsciously
making the statement, "I will NOT be ignored."

LEATRICE EISEMAN, COLOR PSYCHOLOGIST, DIRECTOR OF THE PANTONE
COLOR INSTITUTE AND AUTHOR OF *COLORS FOR YOUR EVERY MOOD*

A wife of noble character who can find?...she is worth
far more than rubies...when it snows, she has no fear for her
household...she is clothed in fine linen and purple.

PROVERBS 31:10,21-22

I n my case, that very first daring step towards truly embracing "The Change" began, in part, with a single bottle of purple nail polish.

I was in my late-forties when I realized I was more than knee deep in the quicksand of perimenopause.

Despite my attempts at controlling symptoms medicinally and herbally, I'd still been down in the dumps for what seemed like months. I was floundering in some seriously deep pools of self-pity—a common temptation for women at this time of life for myriad reasons.

It had started when the first of my four children had headed off to college, and I'd begun to understand that my job description as a wife and mother was beginning to unalterably change. Forever. As each of my kids approached college age, the sensation had become more indomitable in its power over my thinking.

I felt mired down with a fear that I had little, if anything, that would give me the satisfaction and validation I'd felt in my nearly two decades as a type A, overachieving wife and mommy. A girlfriend said it best when she described her own battles with this time period in her life, "It's as though I've just gotten a divorce from my children and it feels like grief."

Worse yet, I was beginning to feel old. Old, stodgy, and fearfully fearful. Long story short, I was hurtling into this thing called The Change of Life and was now eyeball to eyeball with my own mortality.

In tandem with this unsettling seriousness was also the sobering realization that the rest of life didn't look all that fun or inviting anymore. I had to be honest with myself. Despite the fact that I'd been teaching Bible studies off and on for years and even did a short stint as pastor's wife alongside my hubby of nearly three decades, I had a gaping deficit in what the Christian world calls "the fruit of the Spirit." This is the manifest that clearly says that "joy" is an inherent part of God's gift to His kids. Like many of my midlife girlfriends, I hadn't felt all that much joy in far too long.

Now, I don't mean I hadn't smiled or *appeared* happy. In fact, most of my friends would probably describe me as a pretty upbeat person. And sometimes hilariously funny—or at least *I* thought so. They'd probably be shocked at my admission that I felt somewhat joyless at the bottom of my core.

I wanted the kind of joy that King David had in 2 Samuel 6 when he danced before the Lord in a skimpy garment called an ephod. I wanted my emotions of joy to be that wildly naked before God (and anyone else who dared to peek in on my personal life and thoughts). I didn't want to care quite so much about what people—especially those with the *most* power in my life: friends, family, neighbors, colleagues, workmates, church-sisters, and yes, even my spouse—thought of me. Nor did I want to be quite so burdened by a backpack loaded with worry and fear, a ridiculous encumbrance I'd taken on long ago by mistakenly dubbing it "mature responsibility." Like David, I was ready for a step into the unknown. A step into radical, heaven-fueled joy.

What made things seem even bleaker was that when I looked around at most of my peers, which included your average mix of both churchy and nonchurchy folk, EVEN the ones who looked "all-together" didn't seem to have too much of that joy-stuff, either. Things had been way too serious and way too predictable for way too long.

It was then that one of my earliest Hot Flashes from Heaven hit me in the cosmetic department of Wal-Mart.

"So quit staring at it and buy the purple nail polish. It's less than two bucks. How painful can THAT be?"

Now, I know a lot of women whose God speaks to them in eloquent Scripturelike revelations, complete with chapter and verse. And yes, He's done that for me as well. But normally, my relationship with God's voice has always been a lot more primal; more like, well, if I do say so myself, a Hot Flash from Heaven.

I'll hear that soft, warm voice radiate across my soul like a rosy blush, and as it does, it'll sometimes pop off with something totally non-spiritual, like, *"Fix that special casserole tonight."* Then, kaboom, when I'm obedient, I unexpectedly have company for dinner or some other seeming coincidence that has convinced me over my more than 30 years of being friends with Him that there are *no* coincidences when God speaks and man (or woman) listens. At any rate, I've come to feel that God uses simple instructions like *"make a casserole"* so that my far-too-busy writer's mind can more easily believe Him when I hear that same still, small voice whisper simple little words like, *"I love you, Daughter."*

Anyway, hearing Him encourage me to buy that purple polish wasn't all that big of a deal. Buying the polish *was*.

First of all, I felt downright silly at the cash register as the even older cashier checked me out—both literally and figuratively. As she eyeballed me up and down, I felt like screaming back a raging lie to her, "Yes, I know I'm *this* old and, yes, I know *this* color is far too flashy for an old coot like me. This polish, you idiot, is for my 12-year-old granddaughter." Only I didn't have a granddaughter. Didn't even have an engaged kid at the time. And, besides, God probably doesn't like it when we lie and scream and call people idiots while we're trying to follow His leading.

So I just handed the nice lady the money and tucked the paper sack surreptitiously under my arm—as if to hide it—and quickly headed for the door. I felt like a 16-year-old who'd just managed to buy some wildly forbidden beverage at the liquor store with fake ID.

At home I stared at the bottle sitting in front of me. What on earth had I been thinking? Women my age don't wear polish this color.

"Put it on," I heard another whisper gently. *"It ain't called The Change for nothin', honey."*

"Yeah, right," I wanted to snap back at the very thought of actually embracing something that sounded so terrifyingly transforming, but I could tell by the tone of the voice resonating in my thoughts that no one was playing games here.

I cracked open the bottle and layered the purple stuff on. As I did, I chuckled to myself. My hands, which had begun to look more and more like my mother's each day, no longer did. Sweet but all-too-sensible Mom would never have been caught dead in the stuff I was spreading on my nails.

She, like so many elderly women in her peer group, had long ago fallen for the fable that it's far better off to be safe than sorry. In doing so, I'd watched many of their lives, and even a lot of their joy, become incrementally swallowed up by anxiety, fear, worry, and fretfulness.

Safe-little by safe-little step, these adorably aging women's worlds had closed in around them, sealing out potential new friends, adventures, and a big chunk of life. Sure, many of them *still* had passions—like my mom, who loves nothing more than reading a good book late into the night, trying a new recipe out on her revolving door of grandchildren and great-grandchildren, and loving and nurturing without restraint her rapidly growing family tree. But most all of what she did, like so many women of her generation, was done in service to someone else. I wanted to be like that. She'd set an incredible standard for me as her daughter. But I also wanted more. A lot more.

Certainly I wanted to emulate my mom's legacy of unconditional love and service to family. But I didn't want to lose myself—or my excitement over every minute of life—in the process. I wanted to be a bigger, better, brighter *me* in my final years than I had been in my younger ones.

I held my hands out in front of me and admired the iridescence. I felt a little like King David must have felt when he looked at himself clad only in that flimsy little ephod. But that was before he danced before the Lord.

Now to better understand what came next, you need to know a little more about me. Bear with me here. This is about daring midlife steps into The Change, remember?

I had been riding behind my husband on his Harley-Davidson (H-D) motorcycle for about five years. Even that small gesture had been a deep departure from what Mom would have ever done. While I'd at first been terrified, I found a little Xanax, a whole lot of my old childbirth deep-breathing techniques, and meditating on 2 Timothy 1:7: "God has not given us a spirit of fear and timidity, but of power, love, and self-discipline" (NLT), slowly transformed me into a moderately relaxed passenger.

And I emphasize the words *moderately relaxed*. I was still, at my core, terrified of riding. I also realized that my fear of riding was a more-than-accurate metaphor for my approach to aging and life in general.

But on the upside of the fear thing, I discovered that the posture of sitting spread eagle behind my husband and chatting over his shoulder was a miraculous intimacy enhancer to a double-decade marriage that had been in short supply of intimacy for far too long. For some reason, this much closeness to the one I married so many years ago gave me a glimpse into a world I longed to conquer; one of joyful, love-filled, courageous, contagious security. One without fear of anything—much less my spouse, loved ones, or the life we all shared.

The vision was fleeting, however. The year before I found myself putting the purple polish on my fingernails, Bill had talked me into learning to ride my own motorcycle.

Once again I was back to square one on the learning curve of raging terror. I dropped, kicked, and, yes, even cursed that motor-cycle at least 20 times. And forget Xanax. Valium and five margaritas wouldn't have quelled the panic this bike triggered in me. Despite the fact that I put 7000 miles on that red beast that year, I'd hated that bike—and the fear it inspired—from the get-go. I was *NOT* a happy camper. Joy was nowhere on my radar screen. In my worst moments, I thought old-stodgy-fearful-and-predictable a very safe place to return to.

But the next year—the year of the purple polish—I decided to push the envelope of old age one last time before waving the white flag of surrender and climbing back onto my husband's passenger seat for good. This was not long after I had heard that prophetically mysteri-ous voice on the radio station (the one I referred to in my previous chapter) say the word "menopause."

"I think I should try a different bike before I give up altogether," I said to my husband meekly one morning. "I'd like to order a new Harley, a Heritage Softail model. I think the big tire in front might make it easier for me to balance it."

"Fine," answered Bill, appearing ever so calm. He wasn't fool-ing me. Up until this time in our lives, my husband had rarely been calm about spending money—no matter what the amount—and it had been a source of fear-generating, joy-sucking, intimacy-busting conflict for us all our married years.

Some of it was a *self*-imposed fear of my husband—of those often grumpy responses I'd get when I'd have to ask him for either his time or his money and the questions they raised in my own mind about my value as a wife, mother, and homemaker. Did he approve of me and the work I did as caretaker of our home? Did he think *my* work was as valuable as *his* work? Did he think *I* had value—as much value as *he* had? Or did he not?

My misguided desire to please my husband at all costs was something I've now found I share with many of the recovering-June-Cleaver-wannabe's of my generation—no matter what the issues have been in our marriages. The fact that this desire is often carefully veiled under the spiritually confusing misnomers of "submission" and "respect" in the Christian side of some of our lives makes it even trickier to question and challenge.

But that's precisely where The Change comes in.

In my floundering attempts to be the biblically perfect, obedient wife, I'd allowed my husband virtually free rein in far too many of our marital decisions: What we did with our time, how we spent our money, how we prioritized our needs and wants, how close our relationship was. Or wasn't.

Somewhere in the process of life, Ronna Snyder—and her ability to think and dream and feel unabashed joy and courage—had disappeared. She was lost within the lines of a bizarrely distorted caricature of the Proverbs 31 woman. If you're not familiar with her, she's the biblical superbabe who could have easily sung about bringing home the bacon far before those words ever became popular in our culture or chart-busting lyrics to a song back in the 1970s.

I was she. She was I. Whatever. I was that woman in all her full-blown, whacked-out glory. A workaholic wife, endlessly toiling to try to win my husband's approval and always feeling that I'd come up short. Entangled around that thorniness was an even larger serpent—the one my dear mom's generation of women had dealt with for far too long—that equally self-imposed fear of life in general that had all but choked out joy.

"Put in an order for a black one," said my husband, as if by rote. "The color will make it easier to resell if you decide you can't ride it." In his mind, he wouldn't need to face this issue—or its price tag—for another two more years.

You see, anyone who knows anything about Harley-Davidson knows that years ago they developed (bless their rumbling little hearts) an amazing marketing hook for enticing middle-aged males into spending copious amounts of money on something their wives might likely frown upon.

They discovered something women have known since the beginning of time. Just tell a man he can't have something he really, really wants for two years, and he'll want it even more—and pay even more for it—when he gets it. Guys fall for this nearly every time. Thus Harley's once-infamous waiting list and reputation for their sometimes hard-to-get bikes. As a full-fledged member of the estrogen-powered gender, I opted out on allowing a motorcycle dealer to do the same thing to me.

"I bet I can have one by tonight," I replied to my husband. Simple as that little sentence was, it was probably one of the most daring things I'd ever said to the man, and not because of any arbitrary sales policy that Harley had contrived. My husband's power over money in our relationship had left little room for my own, and to tread into that territory was like walking into the mouth of the proverbial lion. Nevertheless, after he left for work I made a phone call to an H-D salesman who'd had my husband on repeated waiting lists for the numerous new Harleys he'd bought over the years.

"Frank," I explained in my very sweetest, I-need-a-knight-to-come-to-my-rescue voice, "you know that used bike Bill bought for me last year? I can't ride the thing—it scares the pudding out of me. I'm going to give up driving my own motorcycle unless…" I paused, trying to make my plea as dramatic as possible, "unless, if by some miracle, you can come up with a brand-new black Heritage Softail by tonight. I *just know* you can find me one. If *any salesman* in America can do this for me, you can, *Frank*." My voice was kissing his feet. "And to prove my confidence in you, I have a $100 tip for you." Mentally, I filed away that I'd have to rob my tightly managed grocery allowance for that $100—but the leading to buy the bike seemed like such a, well, God-thing that I just had to do it.

"Tonight?" Frank questioned feebly.

"Tonight," I replied emphatically. I was a woman on a mission. I had no idea what it was, but somewhere in there, there *had* to be a Hot Flash of insight. As the months and years would wear on after that, I would find out there would be many of them.

But first, there was the phone call that would ring that afternoon.

"I found you a bike," said Frank. Minutes later, after I broke the news to my astounded husband, I got another Hot Flash from Heaven. It settled in on me rapidly, like a souped-up cycle's chromed-out exhaust pipe coming to life when the engine's just been turned on. *"This is just the beginning, Daughter. Your loved ones won't break and your marriage won't topple if you use the brains I gave you, the heart I put in you, and simply assert yourself and reclaim your God-given joy. Life won't end. In fact, it will do just the opposite, if you dare to change. You are of value, Dear One."*

"What?" I wanted to scream back. Change? Assert myself in areas of my life that needed assertion? Act as though I had value? And yet I'd done it.

In claiming ownership on a bike I'd yet to get my husband's approval on, I'd gone somewhere I'd never gone before in my life and marriage. But it didn't feel like (gasp) rebellion. It felt like...what were the words? It felt like...change! It felt fearless. Secure. Maybe even a tad...joyful? And there was certainly no denying my husband's bewildered response later that evening. It was so benign it virtually confirmed to me that my impulsive-appearing actions might truly be God led after all.

"Really?" my husband said when I told him that night that I was the soon-to-be-owner of a new motorcycle and I had no idea how it would be paid for. There were no temper tantrums. No rages. No threats. Just calm acceptance as he methodically got my old bike ready to be sold and cut a check for the new one. It was then my turn to be astounded, as I observed that perhaps Dr. Phil really *is* right when he says, "You teach people how to treat you." When I put on quiet confidence with my husband—even if I was, for the time being, pretending—he responded accordingly, with equally calm respect. I was beginning to change the steps in my lifetime-long dance of deference with a loved one and darned if he didn't join in!

That shiny new black machine, which I only dropped once, helped both of us over several major midlife hurdles that are often part of this time called The Change. Some of them were marital. We began spending more and more time together in the shared interest of riding motorcycles. As a result, intimacy—that thing that only grows in the greenhouse of time spent together—began to take root in our relationship. But most of the changes were internal and personal. I began to see fear for what it really is—a big, fat, joy-robbing lie.

Not so surprisingly, the $20,000 *black* purchase was only the precursor to that explosively radical step when I bought the $2 bottle of *purple* polish. By that day in Wal-Mart I'd already owned the black bike for just a little over two months.

While it had started a paradigm shift in my approach to fear and my search for joy—in, and out of, my marriage—the grape-colored goo was about to kick it up a whole 'nother notch. My confidence was on the cusp of soaring right along with my engine's rpm's.

While I flew, eaglelike, along the highways, I found myself thinking about all the ways that joy-draining fretfulness can monopolize a middle-aged woman's life. We can worry about our kids, our health, our kids' health, our husband (or lack thereof), his health, our marriage (or lack thereof), and our marriage's health. You get the picture. The list can be endless for the midlife mind run menopause-ly amok.

But on the bike I discovered something many of us learn at this fork in the road. We clearly *do* have choices. We can *choose* to *not* fear the fear. Not fret the fretting. Not worry about the worrying. We can *choose* to *change*.

Mastering that 800-lb. hunk of metal taught me a lot about these mental choices that begin to confound women in middle age. Do we let our minds and relationships stay in the status quo simply because we're too terrified to change ourselves or ask for change from others? Or do we, like riding a motorcycle, shift into another gear and go full throttle into embracing a joyful freedom from the fear of change? God used a machine that had more power than many grown men are comfortable riding to empower me in *all* areas of my life.

But there was just one teensy problem. And it goes back to that choice thing *and* the prompting I got looking at that purple nail polish that day in Wal-Mart. Every time I passed a purple bike, I'd twist my neck around to watch it go by.

Why hadn't I risked everything and bought what I would have really chosen if I'd dared to be brave and voice my own opinion? Why hadn't I bought what I'd really wanted—a purple bike? If I had, it would have been the exact color of this fingernail polish, I realized, staring at the bottle that was now in front of me. I mentally kicked myself over and over for being so afraid of being "disobedient" to my husband that I couldn't even voice my own thoughts by saying, "You know, honey, I'd really prefer purple over black." And then, as I watched the purple polish transform my hands—and my mind—another confounded Hot Flash hit.

"Buy a purple bike."

"My black bike is just a couple months old—wassup with that, God? And I thought You led me to buy that one," I almost railed. "Doesn't my husband's calm acceptance prove it? Haven't I learned my lesson well enough?"

How dare God ask me to go back into the desert I'd just come out of and, once again, overcome any remaining fear of dealing with my husband on equal turf.

"Buy a purple bike," I heard again. I was getting no sympathy at all. God was talking to me as though I was an adult, a woman of value,

not a child. *What a novel idea,* I thought to myself. I knew that the next thing I would do would take more bravery than climbing on any motorcycle. I picked up the phone and, less than three months after getting the black motorcycle, once again dialed my H-D salesman.

"Uhhhh, Frank, I know this is going to sound crazy but…"

I, who daily deal in words to make a buck or two, was stumbling all over mine. Might as well just spit it out.

"I just bought some purple nail polish, and maybe it's just a menopause thing, but I want a bike that will match it." Even as I write the words, I know how impulsively spoiled they sound. But, again, there was that blasted Hot Flash throwing caution to the wind and slaying internal trepidation and joylessness right and left.

Silence.

"Frank, are you still there?"

Now it was Frank's turn to verbally stumble as he mentally processed my bizarre request. Suffice it to say, within 24 hours I had a big, burley, purple Harley-Davidson Road King on its way—with, once again, no means to pay for it.

Before you judge me the quintessential spendthrift, you need to know another personal thing about me—about us—about my husband and me. I'd shopped thrift stores and day-old bread stores for more than two decades so that my husband could work half the year as a contractor. The other half of the year we followed *his* dreams, building two ranches and a wilderness hunting lodge that were the envy of all his friends. All three places were his dreams, not mine. And that was fine. I was his helpmate, right? I felt—and still *do* feel—honored to be in that role with a man I madly, dearly love.

At the same time, we'd bankrolled four college educations for our kids, kept ourselves totally debt free, and built up a sizeable retirement account. We were enormously frugal, but we were hardly impoverished. The problem had never been that we had no money. It was simply that my husband controlled virtually all of it—and I'd allowed it, out of the insecure fear of his anger or rejection. While other couples might struggle with different issues, this one had become our marital nemesis of titanic proportions. It was time for a showdown.

"Guess what I did today, honey?" I said as cheerfully and bravely as I could. I swallowed the cantaloupe-sized lump in my throat and said, "I ordered a purple Road King."

The traffic on the highway screeched to a halt. Like a deer in headlights, I dared not blink as I looked deep into the eyes of my massive 6' 1" husband.

And then you know what happened? Absolutely nothing. I was more stunned than *any* deer in *any* headlight. When I'd dared to stare down the thing I'd feared the most, it had vanished like a ghost in the night. I *did* have more power over fear than I'd ever given myself credit for!

Over the years that have followed, the color purple has become my menopausal mantel. It represents to me the ultimate weapon of mass destruction against fear: God-given joy. The purple nail polish, which I now almost always wear either on my toes or my hands or both, is a self-reminder of who I am before God, whether I'm on my Harley or not. In Ronna's rendition of The Change, I've filled my motorcycle wardrobe with outrageous orchid-colored leathers and accessories. In my town I'm now known as "The Purple Lady."

But few people know or understand the reasons behind this midlife color connection, despite my bike's license plate, which reads "Ht4God" (Hot for God). Like the Old Testament guy Mordecai, who proudly wore the purple robes of royalty in the book of Esther, I've begun to proactively don the belief system that I need not have fear for my household—or the relationships within them.

I'm now consistently aware that the same Proverbs 31 woman that I'd wrongly equated with a church mouse was so bold in believing in her own value before God and mankind that the Bible says of her: "She is worth far more than rubies...when it snows, she has no fear for her household...she is clothed in fine linen and purple" (Proverbs 31:10,21-22). As I ride on my bike side by side with my husband, the once-illusive concept of mutual value and equality has not only taken wings in my husband's mind, but also, more important, in my own.

More than once I've had middle-aged women admire my motorcycle and the crazy purple getups I wear while riding it. "I could *never* ride one of those," they'll say wistfully. "I'd be too afraid."

If you only knew, I always think to myself. And oftentimes, as a result, I find myself opening up to perfect strangers about what the bike and this midlife juncture have taught me about fear and my own queenly worth in this universe. I encourage them to take their own daring steps toward change. *And,* I assure them, *you don't need a motorcycle to do it.*

"Pick your own vehicle for change," I urge, "whether it's going back to college, changing careers, reinventing relationships, picking up a new hobby, or even dragging your hubby off to a marriage counselor. Don't run from what could ultimately put a long-lost, God-given, joy-charged smile on your face."

Oftentimes as I'm sharing with other women, those Hot Flashes return and warm me with their tender reminders. *"It's really not called The Change for nothin', honey. You are of value, Daughter, and while others may not understand it, I've used the extravagant fun of a purple Harley to prove to you that, like the Proverbs 31 woman you've always yearned to be, you need have no fear for your household. Nor for yourself."*

My reply to God is no longer that cynical, "Yeah, right," but a very different version: "Yeah, Lord, right on!"

Behind that validating interchange resonates the rumble of midlife joy.

● ● ● ● ● ● ● **MENTAL-PAUSE:** ● ● ● ● ● ● ●

Your Vehicle for Change Can Be
Turbocharged with Good Counsel

Has fear left its tire tracks all over your life? Is it a parasite trying to embed itself in your personality and, in the process, suck the joy right out of who you are and who you want to be? Have your hopes, dreams, even your identity—with regard to key relationships in your life—been garaged for far too long?

While my buying that purple polish careened me into courage in many areas of my personal life, the process was greatly ramped up by having a good professional Christian counselor to talk to. And, truth be known, the most daring step I *really* took was when I went to him all on my own—even without my husband's approval or financial assistance.*

The next courageous step I took was when I later insisted that my husband go with me. And, yes, I understand how you're response might be, "Hey, lady, you don't know my husband. He would never do that." I'd have said the same thing before that fateful day I stared him down and assertively repeated over and over (without getting weepy or whiney), "I NEED you to go. Our marriage NEEDS you to go." Lo and behold, he went—albeit grumbling the entire way. He even wound up liking the counselor.

And it was the counselor who smiled sagely when I told him—even before I told my husband—that I'd ordered a purple Harley. It was also the counselor who taught me how to dissect my perspectives, discerning truth from lies and realizing that fear resides in a house of cards. Take down one card by speaking the truth into a situation, he explained, and the whole thing begins to topple.

---

* If money is an issue in your marriage as well, check your insurance policy to see if it will cover mental health counseling. Your marriage DOES affect your mental health, doesn't it? If you're not covered by insurance, look for a counselor with a "sliding scale"; that is, their charges are scaled to your income. My counselor charges one percent of a person's gross annual income if they are not covered by insurance. That means if you make $40,000 a year, you pay $40.00—a small price for a pathway to peace of mind!

For instance, after nearly a quarter of a century of marriage, I told my husband that in order for me to feel joyful security in our marriage (that level of security is the antithesis of fear), we needed to address issues of money and control in our marriage. But in order to assert myself in what was once such a volatile topic, I had to continually tell myself that God thought I had the same value as my husband. No more, but certainly no less. As I walked in the strength of that truth, my husband, amazingly, followed suit.

If you have joy-robbing, fear-inducing issues you've been dodging up until this time in midlife when you're at the crossroads of change, I encourage you to seek out a wise and caring counselor to help you. If you're married and feel that your husband needs to go as well, keep that in mind as you search for someone you think he would respond to. But don't wait for your husband to gleefully join you. Just go on your own, if need be. It will likely empower you enough to eventually get your husband there. And if he never goes, it'll at least help you deal with that issue as well.

And remember, one size does NOT fit all with regard to counselors. If you don't find someone you have a rapport with, continue "counselor shopping" until you do.

3

Looking for the Lighthouse of Clear Thinking

It's got to be here somewhere in this fog of forgetfulness.

• • • • • • • • **POWER SURGES** • • • • • • • •

Pain of mind is worse than pain of body.

LATIN PROVERB

I have come into the world as a light, so that no one who believes in me should stay in darkness.

JOHN 12:46

One of the bad things about this thing called menopause is that you begin to forget stuff.

Such as where you left $300 worth of groceries in Costco when you got sidetracked looking at the store's new shipment of men's shirts. Yup. Did it a few years back.

This "meno-phenom" often is described ever so kindly as "memory lapses" on the list of symptoms that middle-aged women can experience as their internal gas tanks slowly run out of estrogen.

But in my world it's called "brain fog." I've never heard a single middle-aged woman say, "Oh, I'm so sorry I forgot to make dinner tonight. I've had a memory lapse." Yeah, right. But I have heard a ton of them say "brain fog." And we *all* know what *that* means.

But here's the good news about getting older. You begin to forget stuff.

I kind of like it that way. Brain fog can sometimes be a handy little cocoon to wrap one's own aging fallibilities up in. Did you just honestly forget that important meeting with the advisory board of that nonprofit you donate your time to? (Which I, incidently, did just last week.) Blame it on hormone-shortage-induced brain fog.

After all, your female peer group is either going through it, will be going through it, or *has* gone through it. And they'll usually understand. Unless, of course, they've, uh, forgotten that they occasionally have bouts of brain fog themselves.

But where I've found this forgetfulness both a blessing and a bane is when I have to ask myself a serious question and I really can't remember the answer. Like, "When *did* I get this brain fog?"

Brain fog or no brain fog, I clearly remember the first time I experienced it and I wish I could forget it. It's that embarrassing.

It was a supposedly normal shopping day at Costco. (Yeah, I know, I spend a lot of time there. I happen to love the place. Thus, I have a lot of Hot Flashes from Heaven there.) I'd been in the store for about an hour and, since a few of my kids were still mostly at home (although perched on the edge of the nest and ready to spread their wings any day now), I was filling up a mondo-cart full of mondo-groceries.

You know why faithful customers call Costco "The hundred dollar store," don't you? Because you can easily go in it to pick up, say, a $6 stick of their fabulous summer sausage, and by the time you've made it to the cash register, you've found enough cool stuff to buy that it's doubtful you'll get out of there for less than $100. In my case, Costco's always been the three hundred dollar store.

And it was no different that day. My cart was absolutely stacked to its limit with groceries as I was heading toward the checkout counter.

I might add that I had no kids to distract me. My shopping list was completely checked off. And then I saw them: Way cool men's shirts displayed on a couple of those double-high racks they sometimes put stuff on in the middle of the clothing section of the store. I was totally entranced ("trance" being the pertinent part of that word).

Anyway, before I knew it I was looking at those shirts. With four males in my household, I honestly did more shopping for men's clothes than women's back in those days, so I'd never deliberately drive my Costco cart right past a new shipment of men's shirts.

By the way, they do that on purpose. I've personally heard the CEO of the place talk about how much they love to make a shopping experience in Costco like a treasure hunt—just so you'll never know what you'll find in their ever-revolving slew of top-of-the-line inventory. So let's just say I'd found another Costco treasure trove. It at least makes my next action sound semi sane.

I started looking through the men's shirts—all in sizes my four big guys could wear. Sounds normal, right? Certainly. No problem thus far.

Except for the blackout. The blackout-like shroud of brain fog that made me forget where I left my cart. Or when I left my cart. Or what was in my cart. Or—it gets worse—even what store I was in.

When I emerged from between those two tall racks of men's shirts, I could no more remember the answer to any of the above four sentences than find a lighthouse in heavy fog. Honest.

I looked around. Okay, looks familiar. I vaguely remember this place. Must be Costco. I could at least process that. Heck, with so many kids to feed, I practically lived there. But was I just coming in? I had nothing in my hands to indicate I'd bought anything. Or was I just leaving? How long had I been in there? And if I had already picked some things up, where on earth were they? It was similar to parking your car in the parking lot and then going back out and totally forgetting where you'd parked it. Everyone can identify with that. I mean, this doesn't make me insane, does it?

But who loses a full cart of groceries in Costco? This seriously scared me. Now I was beginning to think I was not just entering the menopausal years, but I had Alzheimer's on top of it!

I would soon learn I am not alone. But back to that cart of groceries. I started v-e-r-y s-l-o-w-l-y retracing the steps I couldn't remember. Like a fog burning off in the first rays of sunlight, it all began, e-q-u-a-l-l-y s-l-o-w-l-y, to come back to me. I had been on my way out of Costco. "Yes, yes, that's right," I tried to encourage myself. I now remembered that part. (Mostly because my mind had just given me a dim recollection that I'd walked into the store.) So I just walked up and down the aisles (being careful to not get distracted again) until I found a very full cart at the front of the store, unattended, and not far away from the men's shirts. I looked at the contents. I recognized things I'd needed. It was all coming back to me. Finally.

And then there was the time I misplaced $2000 in cash. But I have a good excuse here. I was distracted, okay? Oops, that's the one I used in the preceding parable. Anyway, my daughter was in town to visit, and it was the holiday season. She and I made a run to my bank to cash a nice-sized check for a laundry list of Christmas grocery and gift shopping.

I adore my daughter. When I see her, which isn't nearly enough since she now lives in an entirely different state than I do, I see the good in me. I'm thrilled that she got some of my better DNA, and not the hormonal, whacked-out, brain fog part (at least thus far). As a result I absolutely love chatting with her. And so that's what I was doing as I stuffed 20 $100 bills deep into my secret pocket in my wallet. *I'll never lose it here,* I said to myself. We chatted some more as we drove on to do what we girls do best together: shop.

Fifteen minutes later we were in Wal-Mart, another store I also have a lot of Hot Flashes from Heaven in. I reached into my wallet to pull out the money. (This was back in my "pay only in cash" days. Events like this have forced me to ditch the cash and pay only with plastic.) It was gone. In 15 minutes I'd lost $2000! And we'd never even gotten out of the car until we arrived at Wal-Mart!

I panicked. My daughter panicked. I tore my wallet apart. I couldn't find the money. I unloaded my entire purse (not an easy task because I use it like a footlocker for makeup). It wasn't there, either. I rushed back to my daughter's car and looked over, under, and in between the seats. I looked on the concrete outside the car. Maybe it had fallen out when I'd exited the car? Nothing. I retraced my steps through Wal-Mart. No sign of it there. I went to customer service and confessed my stupidity and begged that they'd call me if they found that one person left on the planet who was honest enough to turn in $2000 in cash just a couple weeks before Christmas. Then I did what I should have done in the first place. I prayed. My daughter prayed. That night when I was forced to tell my husband, he prayed, but not before I got a sermon about how crazy it is to try to carry $2000 in cash.

When the money still hadn't been found by that following week, I told the gals in the Bible study I taught at a homeless shelter about the incident and asked them to all pray. (Of course, I didn't tell them how much I'd lost. Their response to my loss would have likely been, "Welcome to my world, girfriend.") And every week after that I continued to pray until I faced the grim reality. The money was truly gone. It had disappeared into another episode of cataclysmic cerebral smog.

Two months later, long after the holidays were over, I was doing a freelance story for one of my magazine clients. It involved not just writing the piece but also shooting the photography for it. The subject of the article requested my business card. I went out to the car to retrieve one from my purse that was safely locked in the trunk. When I pulled it out, I couldn't find my business cards, either.

I am getting so totally sick of this, I thought to myself as I remembered my recent $2000 loss. If Jesus is the light of the world, the least He could do would be to shine a little of it into the fading brain cells in my own cranium.

Sheeez, I added, *I just know those business cards have got to be in here somewhere.* I dug deep in the wallet pocket where I normally keep them. And I felt a lump. It was bigger than the one that was quickly forming in my throat. Could it be? Could it be? I clawed at the lump until out spilled 20 $100 bills! I was thunderstruck. It was in a pocket I'd looked in at least ten times! How could this be? Amid my "Thank You, thank You, thank You, Jesus," I began to tremble at the thought that whatever was happening in my head just might be terminal. At the time, I didn't know it had a name. But by the end of the day, I'd discovered it on a menopausal Internet bulletin board: Brain fog—another one of menopause's dirty little secrets.

So I started bouncing the two words off a few of my midlife girl-friends. One by one, they shared tales of experiences similar to mine.

There was my friend Becky. She was in her mid-forties. That was about the only thing we had in common at the time. She's the polar opposite of me. A left-brained, analytical thinker. A nuts-and-bolts kinda gal. Extremely serious. Pokerfaced. And she was even more so when she confided to me her most frightening fog.

She was driving down city streets she'd driven daily for decades. And then a couple little questions hit her: Does "red" mean "stop"? Or does "red" mean "go"? Or is it green? And then it got worse. She couldn't remember if she was supposed to drive on the left side of the road. Or was it the right side?

She quickly scanned the cars surrounding her and determined that she was indeed in the correct lane of traffic since she was going the same direction they were, but she was majorly freaked out by the experience. And like me in Costco, it slowly came back to her. *Uh-huh, sweetie, red means stop; green means go.* It left her shaken for days. That is, until she visited her doctor and he prescribed a hormonal patch that quickly helped dissipate the fog. Months later, she could actually laugh about it, even though she's not the laughing type.

Shawna's story of brain fog was even more outrageous. She'd come home from grocery shopping, unpacked everything, and got dinner ready to go, sticking the chicken in the oven and setting the timer. Then she put the salad vegetables in the crisper to stay cold.

When her husband arrived home from work, hours later, she reached into the crisper to whip her green salad together. Only the vegetables weren't *in* the crisper drawer. They weren't even in the refrig-erator.

Where could they be, she asked herself. She looked in the car. Maybe she'd left them in the car? Then she looked on her cupboard shelves. Could she have misplaced them there? Finally, in complete desperation, she looked in the freezer. The crisper drawer she'd thought she'd put her vegetables into was actually a freezer shelf. The lettuce, tomatoes, celery and other fresh veggies were now frozen solid.

Things were not looking too good for poor Shawna, who was about 45 at the time and experiencing her first bout of full-blown brain fog. She was scrambling as to how she could resurrect the frozen veggies into some kind of stir-fry with the chicken.

The chicken! Shawna panicked. She couldn't smell chicken baking. She literally *ran* to the oven and opened it. She'd set the timer for the following day! The oven hadn't even started! But Shawna was overwhelmed with relief. Why?

Because she'd put the entire chicken, Styrofoam tray, cellophane wrap and all, in the oven.

Makes my missing cart in Costco and missing money in Wal-Mart sound like a slightly saner, and safer, form of brain fog, huh?

I can hear you now. "Quick, Ronna! I'm suffocating in brain fog! I need to know: What Hot Flash from Heaven got you through times like this? What ethereal words of wisdom calmed you down, soothed your soul, built you up, and pointed you out of this brain smog as surely as a lighthouse in an equally heavy fog?"

Well, here's the deal, girlfriends. I had an incredibly powerful Hot Flash from Heaven that completely explained the wonders of this aging female phenomenon and how to handle it. I know I had at least one. Really, I did. I *must* have. It's in there (in my brain, memory, soul, whatever) somewhere. I just know it is. But...now I expect you to not only understand, but empathize with me, okay? Because I, uh, I, uh, I forgot.

● ● ● ● ● ● ● **MENTAL-PAUSE:** ● ● ● ● ● ● ●

Brain Fog Can *Actually* Illuminate a Pathway Toward a Calmer Life

Sorry about forgetting that Hot Flash from Heaven, but here's what I have figured out about brain fog. Like real fog, it does lift. (And yet, unfortunately, again like real fog, it can drift back in.)

For me, brain fog is often a signal that I've been doing too much. That my brain's on overload and my body is overly tired. As a writer I all too often find my body doing something (like cleaning the kitchen) while my brain is completely somewhere else.

And because brain fog often flies in tandem with hyper-adrenalized anxious thinking, I've made a concerted effort to rein back my brain's tendency toward endless multitasking that's like pouring gasoline on the flames of anxiety.

I get more rest and then focus on quieting the inner mind chatter that can easily create clouds of confusion and worry by:

- Stilling the mind by "looking outside my body"— observing what my hands are doing, really seeing where my feet are going, noticing things like the sweet smell of the air I'm taking in, the feel of the sun on my face—any singular thought that gets me outside my head.

- S-l-o-w-ing down thoughts, movements, and self-talk. Methodically doing everything more slowly and with more concentration on simply what I'm doing right there in that moment.

- Listening for the inner voice of God to guide my steps as its gentle simplicity shines an enormous light on fog-filled thinking.

- Staying focused on only the task at hand and giving it as an offering to God—no matter how small and insignificant it might seem.

I will add a caveat here. Brain fog and anxiety can be signs of depression. If there's any possibility that you might be depressed (after all, you are in peri- or full-blown menopause), you might want to take the depression self-test below and, depending upon what you find out about yourself, see a trustworthy counselor and/or compassionate physician for some extra help—pharmaceutical or otherwise.

According to the U.S. National Institute of Mental Health (NIMH), some of the main symptoms and signs of depression are the following:

- Persistent sad, anxious, or empty mood
- Feelings of hopelessness, pessimism
- Feelings of guilt, worthlessness, helplessness
- Loss of interest or pleasure in hobbies and activities that were once enjoyed, including sex
- Decreased energy, fatigue, being slowed down
- Difficulty concentrating, remembering, making decisions (brain fog)
- Insomnia, early morning awakening, or oversleeping
- Appetite and/or weight loss or overeating and weight gain
- Thoughts of death or suicide; suicide attempts
- Restlessness, irritability
- Persistent physical symptoms that do not respond to treatment, such as headaches, digestive disorders, and chronic pain

4

Refeathering Your Nest

Plucking out guilt and depression and hatching the new you in midlife.

I looked on child rearing not only as a work of love and duty, but as a profession that was fully as interesting and challenging as any honorable profession in the world and one that demanded the best that I could bring to it.

ROSE KENNEDY

Train up a child in the way he should go, and when he is old he will not depart from it.

PROVERBS 22:6 NKJV

I first noticed the fallen nest on one of my daily forays to my horse barn. For days I passed by it, wedged on its side in the barn's soft sand. I never looked inside. In my almost half century of living I'd seen plenty of emptied nests. They no longer held any magic for me.

But one day I ventured to touch it. Squatting down to its level, I set it upright in the dirt and marveled at the signature left behind by its builder. A solitary aqua egg lay cushioned in the abandoned nest. The fact that it had fallen from the wind-ravaged rafters fifteen feet above and somehow survived the chaotic tumble with the egg still intact spoke to me. Had this nest been built and then dropped, like a message straight from the mouth of God, just for me?

Gently I picked it up, cradled it in my cupped hands, and carried it back to the house. As I did, a Hot Flash from Heaven crept as delicately as that egg's shell into my thoughts.

"Empty nests are actually viewing platforms from which human moms can prayerfully watch their hatchling-children take flight. In doing so, these women also launch themselves into a new, more powerful, form of motherhood," it whispered. *"Examine the nest in your hands. You'll learn much from it, and in doing so, you'll birth a new you."*

As I did, I marveled at how the mother robin had created her children's home. The first interior layers of the nest were fluffy with down and softly woven with dried grasses. If birds feel love, I could picture the mama bird feathering the foundation of her nest, much as I had done nearly a quarter of a century ago when pregnant with the first of our four children.

I thought on how she and I had each labored to build our nests, and I reflected upon my own early years of motherhood. Raising little ones had seemed so easy then. Their "Mommy, how come…?" questions seemed as light of a responsibility as this nest's base. They believed everything I said. Mommy and Daddy were always right. God was good. Life was simple. They trusted in everything we taught them.

But then they grew up. Into teenagers and beyond.

Little did I know that those first 18 years of their lives would be my easiest years of mothering. Those were the years before they perched on the lip of my nest, surveyed the world around them, and then, chaotically crashing their wings through the air, careened into flight.

In mothering, as in many things in life, ignorance is often bliss. So, like generations of parents—both human and avian—before me, I just kept building the nest's secondary layers. As I did, I remained completely and naively sure that their father and I were crafting a home stout enough to withstand the toughest of storms. How optimistically oblivious I had been!

I studied the nest even more.

Much like me, this feathery mom had dug deep into the mud of life. Piece by spittled piece she'd created, again like me, what she thought was a veritable fortress. The nest in my hands rose majestically with high ridges of daubed clay, and in doing so, its walls had been strong enough to sustain the cataclysmic fall—proof positive that the ol' gal had done a pretty good job.

And here I was: A middle-aged woman, who was now an ol' bird in her own right, with my own nearly emptied nest. I stared into the deep recesses of that bird's domain and heard the questions that befall all mothers when they land on this branch of midlife.

Did I feed my own chicks with the nourishment that would make them strong enough to take flight above the elements?

Did I make my nest walls high enough and rugged enough to protect these now almost-grown children?

Did I teach them by my example that they could soar freely like eagles—free from the baggage of the past? Maybe even free from the baggage of their own parents' errors?

Did I teach them how and where to land safely with wise choices and even wiser decisions?

And, most important, when the time would come to build their own nests, would they remember that I'd tried my best to teach them that the most dependable place to build a home is in the shelter of a tree with deep and spreading roots, roots entwined around a rock so massive that they could never be shaken? Roots entwined around a belief system anchored in a rock-solid God?

"*The egg is your answer,*" said the still, small voice in my head.

Just like the mother bird, there had been storms in my family's life. Seasons I simply couldn't have forecast as a young mom. I had made mistakes. Plenty of them. And so had my husband. Some of them were horrific from my retrospectively repentant viewpoint. We'd been too strict. Put too many demands on the emotions of our kids. Hadn't taught them enough about the sheer fun of living life and how to partake in it—primarily because we were clueless about it ourselves.

In doing so, I agonized over whether we had actually pushed our precious nestlings away from God instead of toward Him, away from joy instead of toward it. My heart was heavy with the knowledge that now that my children were older, some of them still hadn't seemed to have found a firm foundation on which to land. I watched them circling the skies, like anxious young sparrows, looking for a secure place—one without predatory hawks or vultures—where they could build their own nests.

"Over here, over here," I wanted to shout out to them from the rock I was standing on. But my words were swept away by the winds of life, and I knew they were too concerned with their own flight patterns to hear.

I had to remember that God, in His infinite design, had encouraged—maybe even ordained—my husband and me to build that nest anyway.

"You need to be comforted in that," the Hot Flash spoke as serenely to my soul as a bird on the wings of the wind, the voice of a God who is in the business of creating mosaics of perfection out of the broken shells of our human imperfection.

"My Word says simply, 'Raise up a child in the way he should go and when he is OLD, he shall not depart from what you've taught him.' It DOESN'T say WHEN in the aging process that is. But you can still perch on the branch of that promise."

I reasoned with my faith-faltering self and again dared to ask the question that has befallen all the menopausal moms I know. Will my kids be safe in the skies of adulthood? I thought again about that egg.

And then I knew I simply *must* trust that if a mysteriously awesome supernatural power could keep a nest intact during a fifteen-foot fall, that same magnificent mightiness could protect my own human brood. Despite all my flaws. All my errors. All my sin. All my humanness.

If God could spare a single egg in a windstorm, how much more would He care for my own four?

"Let go of the sadness and browbeating," said the downey soft hush in my heart. *"You can now refeather the nest with prayers for your grown children. And their someday spouses. And their future children. And your someday grandchildren; and then, their future grandchildren. All of this is a type of ordained nest building. Trust me, you STILL have much influence in their lives. And much to do as a nest builder. In doing so, you'll hatch this thing I call "a new you" and discover a new form of motherhood."*

Those were difficult words to hear. In many ways, I didn't want to be a *"new you."* And I definitely didn't want a new form of motherhood. I didn't want to be the courageous midlife mom who watches, prays, and trusts from afar. I wanted to be the old, obliviously optimistic, hands-on-mommy. The one who didn't believe I could mess up as a mother. The one who was absolutely, positively convinced I could kiss away all my children's boo-boos.

And I wanted my "old" kids back too. The ones who hung on my every word. Who thought I, in turn, hung the moon. The ones who still hadn't discovered that I was human. And that they were too. And that there are some boo-boos no human being can ever kiss away.

Yet I knew the words were true. It was time to start pecking my way out of the shell of depression and guilt that held me hostage to the past. It was time to trust that the air currents of my prayers really would eventually carry my kids where they were meant to go—no matter what it looked like at the time. It was time to trust that even if *my* nest hadn't been strong enough to prepare my kids for life, God's was.

Tears fell as I stroked the turquoise egg. Moments later I took it back down to the house. I placed it, nest and all, on my kitchen windowsill, where it still remains years later.

The baby of the family, my then-fifteen-year-old, came home that night and eyed the nest suspiciously. With his siblings all growing and mostly gone, he was the youngest hatchling left. Not the least bit impressed with the mother bird's handiwork, he lectured me as only teenagers can.

"Don'tcha know that egg's gonna stink pretty soon and break apart?" he asked, more statement of fact than question.

I looked up at him from the dinner I was making with a motherly but defiant smile. After all, what do kids know about nests? Or about eggs? Or about the self-berating moments of raising a family, letting them go, then agonizing over whether we, as mommies, did our job well enough? What do they understand about the universal struggle of midlife mothers who desperately, prayerfully, try to rest on nestlike viewing platforms as we watch our offspring precariously take flight into the dangerous air of adulthood? Could they possibly ever know how hard it is to let go of "that old mommy within" to trust that God can refeather her into a "new you"? A different kind of mother than was ever imagined back in the diaper days?

"No, it won't," I replied to my 6'5" chick who still thought he knew everything. I felt confident in the answer I gave him as I slipped the casserole into the oven. "This egg won't break. Nor will this nest."

● ● ● ● ● ● ● **MENTAL-PAUSE:** ● ● ● ● ● ● ●

Renesting Can Hatch New Perspectives

Are you grieving at the thought of your children leaving the nest, mourning over what you would have, should have, could have done differently? Let me assure you, there will come a time when you'll be "over it."

There was a point in my journey through this inevitable part of The Change when I'd go to my firstborn's room, empty since he'd left for college, and grab handfuls of the remaining clothing hanging in his closet. I'd shove my nose into them as though I were snorting some illegal drug and smell his unique aroma and think about all the things I could have done differently. Then I'd bawl my heart out. This went on, almost daily, for many months.

But then one day I felt led to do a rather strange thing—something I now highly suggest to anyone whose nest, and heart, is emptying. I "renested." And, in so doing, I cracked open a new way to look at things.

Despite the emotional pull to keep my son's bedroom preserved, almost shrinelike, I went into the place that was beginning to feel more like a tomb and rearranged it. I cleaned it thoroughly, sprinkling in some of my own touches; a new bedspread, fresh curtains, a wreath on the wall. I bought magazines about decorating and design the way I used to do when I was first building my nest and became even more inspired.

I knew I was on the road to recovery when I began eyeing my other kids' rooms, which I knew would be vacant soon as they each went off to college.

My eldest son came home from school that summer, messing up the new bedspread and dumping his dirty laundry in huge piles across my, er, his floor. I walked into the room that I had repossessed and felt instantly annoyed. "This is my space now," I wanted to growl at my son, feeling a little like a hungry lioness guarding her kill.

And then I caught myself as I realized the change my little redecoration and reclamation project had brought to my own perspective. I smiled to myself. This was a new type of motherhood I'd entered. I was actually becoming a new type of mother.

Sure, I would continue to agonizingly pray for my kids. But I had begun to view my son for what he now was—a nearly grown adult who, like me, would try to do the best he could at life, but would sometimes fail and would likely have his own regrets when he reached my age. While I wasn't over the hump yet (I still had three more children to go), I could—at least partially—see that there truly is light at the end of the Big M's sometimes very dark parental tunnel.

When Your Ticking Clock Stops

"Mothering" your "need to mother" when
the mommy meter keeps running.

● ● ● ● ● ● ● **POWER SURGES** ● ● ● ● ● ● ●

Making the decision to have a child is momentous.
It is to decide forever to have your heart go walking
around outside your body.

ELIZABETH STONE

"The woman, seeing that she could not go unnoticed,
came trembling and fell at his feet. In the presence of
all the people, she told why she had touched him and how
she had been instantly healed.

LUKE 8:47

I remember the day as though it were yesterday, but it was just a little over three decades before. I was a young married woman. Twenty-five years old, to be exact. It was 1976. Bill and I had been married less than four months. It was a beautiful sunny day in early autumn, but we could have been in the middle of a bleak winter snowstorm for all I cared. That wouldn't have affected my outlook in the least. In my heart, everything was lit with sunshine.

I was carrying a secret—a secret in my womb—as I walked down Second Street in Spokane, Washington from my doctor's office to pick out a new pair of eyeglasses at my favorite frame shop in town. A blizzard couldn't have hidden the smile that was sweeping across my face as I looked at my sideways reflection in the store windows I was passing. My profile didn't look much different, but, boy, did I feel it.

I walked into the shop and tried on frames, doing my best to look casual. Inside of me, I felt anything but. For I was carrying a secret I couldn't wait to tell. The clerk assisting me was the first to receive it.

"I just found out I'm pregnant," I said to her as I tried my best to sound nonchalant.

"Your first?" she quizzed, preoccupied by the frame selections I was making.

"My first," I replied, knowing that, with those two simple words, my world had just changed forever. I no longer cared in the slightest about buying glasses. I couldn't wait to make my next stop.

A half hour later I walked into our advertising agency, where my husband was busy at his desk. I stood in front of it quietly until he looked up.

"You're going to be a father," I said softly to him. His world, whether he knew it or not, had now also just changed forever.

"Really," he said, more statement of fact than question. As he spoke, he looked up at me and rocked back in his chair. Ever the pragmatist, he made a steeple with his hands, touching his fingers to his lips as if he were contemplating a huge business merger. But then a tiny wisp of a smile crept out of the left corner of his mouth.

"Really," I replied back, softer still. At that point in our marriage, we both had much to learn about expressing our own emotions and then nurturing them in one another. But even that lack of relational development couldn't diminish the power of that day.

Speed scroll through 30 years of marriage and four children.

This time I was in Costco, coincidently again looking at eyeglass frames. Across from me were aisles jam-packed with DVD burners, plasma screens, and 8-billion gigabyte (or something like that) wireless laptops and cell phones that did everything but pick out your wardrobe and floss your teeth. Life had certainly changed, I thought to myself as I perused the merchandise of an entirely new millennium. But in other ways it hadn't.

Here I was again carrying another secret deep down in my womb. But contrary to that glorious fall day so many years ago, the feelings racing through me like a herd of heart palpitations were a far more complicated jumble than the glowing joy I'd once felt.

"Excuse me," I wanted to say to the people pushing carts past me, "Do I look different to you? Because, you see, I think I'm in menopause. I think I may have had my last period. Oh, and did I mention that my youngest child just left the nest six weeks ago?"

Like my reflection in those store windows those many years before, I would pause, turn sideways, and look at my body's profiled image reflecting off Costco's clear glass freezer doors.

Am I different? I wanted to ask the reflection, already pretty sure of the answer. *But how am I different?* I wanted to quiz. *And, more important, will I survive this difference?*

My womb was as silent in its reply as the people I was passing. It was a couple weeks past my period—a period that had never failed to greet me nearly every 28 days of every month that I wasn't pregnant for all of my grown-up life. But this month it had failed to show up.

I know what you might be thinking here, but trust me, I had no concerns about a surprise pregnancy. Bill had taken care of that possibility years before.

Almost no woman enjoys the inconveniences that this time of the month brings, but I was, all of a sudden, missing it terribly. I'd always been one of those rare maternal souls who looked at my menses as a monthly memorial to who I am: Wife. Mom. Full-fledged female.

But this day I was wrestling with a new realization, like that day so many years ago, that my body might just possibly have slipped its internal auto-pilot into a life event much larger than I could ever know—or control.

The temptation to grab a perfect stranger, any woman older than myself, and ask her if she'd survived this time period called "The Change of Life" was almost as strong as the day I shared my first pregnancy with the eyeglass lady. But wisely I held my tongue. I dared not say a thing for fear someone would call the police and they'd haul me away, straightjacketed, with an IV drip of estrogen mainlining into my heart.

Instead I just kept walking through the aisles—aisles that had become so familiar to me over the years of feeding my family of six that most of the employees knew me by name. But this time, like my womb, things were *very* different.

I picked up one of those big frozen lasagna trays, the kind that would have barely fed my clan of half a dozen years before. *Lasagna sounds good,* I said to myself. *Especially if I don't have to make it,* I added smugly. But then I stopped myself. I was no longer feeling smug.

What would I do with all that lasagna? And trite as that silly little question sounds, it rang with profound sadness in the shadows of my spirit. Because the answer to it meant that there were no longer chicks in my nest the size of NBA players that needed to be filled up. My last 6' 5" superstar had rolled out of the driveway more than a month before on his way to a summer job on Washington State's Orcas Island, some 300 miles away.

The unspoken implication? My family, as I'd known it, was gone; and so was my ability to ever procreate another. In that agonizing analysis was something so powerful it hit me like a Hot Flash from Heaven.

"The demise of anything is always the birthplace of something else," I heard, part in warning, part in gentle reassurance, that this, too, might be a preplanned passage.

"And this, rightfully so, is a type of grief. It's okay to feel it—but not forever," it added as if to encourage the emotional mourning sickness I was feeling.

That Hot Flash was way more than I'd bargained for in Costco, but I maintained my composure—at least until I hit the checkout lane.

A young woman in capris and a snug little T-shirt stretching across her expanding midriff was just in front of another middle-aged female customer who was directly in front of me. The young woman looked like a model for one of those flashy new parenting magazines with flickers of the flesh of her pregnancy peeking out from under her T-shirt.

Isn't she adorable, I thought to myself, and then I looked at the woman directly in front of me. She looked a little older, a little further down the midlife trail, than I. She was also keenly eyeing the young mommy-to-be.

The gray-haired gal and I looked briefly at one another as we glanced back at the younger one and then reconnected our eye contact and smiled at each other.

Despite our pleasant faces, my eyes brimmed as hers misted over. My clock might have stopped ticking, but my mommy meter was still on overdrive. "I think I'd give anything to have those days back again," I whispered to her, trying to control my emotions.

She nodded back, biting her lip and trying to hold in her own. She didn't say anything. She didn't need to.

When I got home, I called my girlfriend Tawnya. Packing my portable phone with me as I lugged the things I'd eventually bought at Costco into the house, I described my shopping excursion to her; and then I reminisced about that other day all those years ago. Before I could finish my story, I burst into tears.

"The difference is, Tawnya…" I sobbed, "…the difference is…that back then…being pregnant…was the *beginning* of something. This feels like…like…the *end* of something…the *death* of something."

Seven years younger than me and still menstruating, my clueless friend waited gently and patiently while I wept into the phone.

That night, after the lights were out and he wouldn't have to see my face, I told my husband about the incident. "I-think…that I-think…that I-think…that I want to have another baby," I said into the silence of our bedroom, knowing that while my period was a little late, and just might have stopped forever, that maybe, just maybe, I could squeeze in one last pregnancy. Except for the minor matter of my husband having taken care of that option years before. But I needed to say the words, nonetheless. I needed to at least mull the option over in my mind, one last time, if only to pretend that I still had the choice.

My poor husband did his best to not say the wrong thing and overreact. His trusty vasectomy was doing a marvelous job of keeping him from freaking out.

"Do you really think you'd want to have another baby? At this time in our lives?" he asked as calmly as any man over 50 might at a time like this.

On the one hand I pictured the diapers. The demands. The dedication. The responsibility. The work. And the worry.

On the other hand I remembered the sweet, intoxicating smell of my babies; the joy I'd felt in tending them; the purpose, direction, and devotion I'd felt in raising them. I snuggled into my husband's shoulder and wept with deep, gulping, disgustingly messy—but at the same time—deliverance-delivering sobs.

"I miss my children," I choked out between my tears. "I miss being a 'mommy.'" My bewildered husband held me and rocked me.

A few days later the phone rang. As opposed to that sunny, autumn day 30-some years before, the weather was about as fittingly overcast and drizzly as what my gynecologist was about to say to me.

"It's as you suspected, Ronna," he said. "You're in full-blown menopause. Estrogen levels go from 36 to 400. You're at 37—about as low as you can go."

His voice faded into the distance as dozens of thoughts assaulted me at once.

I thought I'd prepared for this day in those years of perimenopause that preceded it. And in some ways I had. There was that purple Harley sitting in my garage that put a smile on my face every time I rode it. There were all those little redecorating projects I'd done in each of the kids' rooms as, one by one, they'd moved out and I'd laid claim, once again, to my space. Those, too, had brought grins to my face and heart. And there was all that marital work my husband and I had done to birth a new type of relationship; one I'd never, not for all the Pampers in the world, turn back the clock on.

Nevertheless, there were those doom-filled thoughts. Negative self-talk like "out of gas," "out of time," "out of eggs," "dried up," and "used up" bombarded me. I hung up the phone. Then, taking advantage of our all-too-empty house, I bawled as loud and as long as I felt like it.

I walked around my home, looking at those rooms once occupied by my kids. And I listened to the silence; a silence I thought I'd grown accustomed to.

"Why am I *still* having such trouble adjusting to this?" I asked into the emptiness, praying for a Hot Flash of insight. None came. Then I remembered the one I'd heard in Costco that day.

"The demise of anything is always the birthplace of something else."

What on earth did that mean? What were the implications of the words "demise" and "birthplace"? I waited, expectantly, for their meaning to jell in my life.

It would take a while for me to figure it out. And the answer would come by way of another one of those Hot Flashes from Heaven.

"You still have birth to give, life to give to others…" it would say on a particularly grim day on my no-longer-hormonal calendar, *"…as you reach out and touch."* The instructions stopped as abruptly as had that final period of mine.

Reach out and touch? Touch what? That confused the spit out of me. But the more I pondered it, the more I realized I needed to tap into people and things that would suck up those reoccurring mommy juices that kept flooding my otherwise drying-up body. I needed to reach out and touch both people and things that would benefit from the way I was wired maternally.

I needed to quit languishing over the loss of 9 x 13 pans of Costco lasagna and instead cook up other things to lay my hands on: Things, and people, that would benefit from my innately female need to nurture. In short, I needed to "mother" my need to mother.

I started small. Literally.

I donated some time to my church's nursery and requested the most demanding challenges—the tiniest babies. There I'd sit, usually flanked by other midlife women who looked as though they were in the same state of desperate mommy withdrawal that I was. We cooed and rocked and nuzzled those precious children through those short stints of time that were just long enough to let me know I simply didn't have the physical or emotional stamina to go the long haul needed to raise another child.

When the younger moms came in to retrieve their newborns, I was surprised to find myself sighing with relief. The next day my shoulders and back would ache from rocking the little darlings. *Hmmmmm,* I said to myself. Mommyhood didn't feel quite as good as I remembered it.

From there I moved on to working in homeless shelters teaching Bible studies; mentoring and mothering women less fortunate than I. There I discovered that "tending and befriending" others plugs into women that same internal maternal power source that infuses us with the need to nurture. And an amazing thing happened. I found that the more emotive energy I expended, the better I felt. The more I touched others, the more touched I became by the sheer joy of life. That quickly began softening the blows of my children leaving home, eliminating those moments of craziness when I was almost duped into thinking I wanted another baby.

There's a reason the Bible states that it's more blessed to give than to receive, and I found that, like raising children, tending to the needs of others takes the obsessive focus off one's own needs. Jesus had it figured out. When He wanted to heal someone, what did He do? He reached out and touched them! When someone needed healing, like the woman in the book of Luke, and they couldn't get Jesus' attention, they reached out and touched *Him,* and then *they* were healed!

Think about it: Touching and being touched has profound implications for the aging.

And then came the flowers.

For the record, I hate gardening. Oops, let me put that sentence in the past tense. I *hated* gardening. So much so that I prided myself on not having a single flower bed in my whole yard. And it's a lot of yard. Out in the country, where I live, a person's yard is only limited by the acreage she owns. It can appear to go on ad infinitum if you own more than 100 acres, and a riding lawn mower, the way we do. So, when we designed and built our dream home ten years ago, it included a massive deck that would accommodate all our entertaining with a sweeping lawn that came right up to it. " Sorry, Charlie." No room or need for flowers.

That was until the insane day I designed my daughter's wedding invitation to invite people to her dream wedding—one she wanted to call a "garden wedding." At our place. The place with no garden.

This put me into a full tilt, wigging out, fertilizing frenzy, all the while praying that the place would, in less than three months, look "sorta" like a garden. All I can say is thank God for alyssum! The delicate-looking, baby's breath-like ground cover spreads like weeds in our clay-filled soil. Its pretty little white and lavender flowers and mesmerizing perfume tricked everybody into believing that I might actually know how to grow something other than children.

During that time of nursing all those infant plants, I found a startling side benefit to getting my nails dirty. Like my experience in the church nursery and homeless shelters, babying those blooms also drained off more of those overabundant mommy juices without me ever having to reverse a vasectomy, adopt a child, or change a diaper.

"Wassup with this?" I quizzed my middle-aged editor girlfriend whose job it is to know answers to almost any question a woman reader—or writer—can ask. And she hit me with a theory she'd recently discovered that rocked my rocker; one she, too, had seen playing out in her own life and those of her fellow middle-aged girl-friends.

She called it "nurturing your need to nurture" as, one by one, she'd seen friends sink their hands into the tactile and emotional stimulation of getting something to grow.

Whether it was a garden like mine or a hunk of clay that needed to "grow into" a pottery bowl, a puppy that needed raising or a colt that needed training, a canvas that needed to mature into a for-real painting or a series of quilt squares that were just itching to be birthed into a full-fledged bedspread, she'd observed that an abundant number of middle-aged women were now procreating in entirely new venues besides childrearing. And for the most part, it was largely tactile. They were touching and being touched! These women were putting their hands to the plow and not looking back.

I looked at all those plants I'd put so much hope and sweat equity into and understood. The demise of my ability to procreate had inseminated in me an insatiable appetite to create (as in lovingly nurture someone or something) and recreate (as in have recreational fun). In putting my own hands to the plow, I found myself turning up oodles of new people and things to love and baby.

My editor friend attributes this to research recently done at prestigious places such as UCLA that links the woman's need to nurture with the profoundly powerful hormone oxytocin. That's the female body's natural tranquilizer, which nukes anxiety and depression. The feel-good stuff floods a woman when she has an orgasm, gives birth, nurses a baby, or cuddles someone or something she dearly loves.

Those in the know state that if you want to nurture your own need to nurture (and receive the positive benefits of having more oxytocin in your body), the best way to do it is to "reach out and touch someone or something" in a loving and caring manner. Thus my maternal bonding with the babies in the church nursery, the "babes" in the homeless shelter, and that bunch of bloomin' blossoms.

Call me an oxytocin junkie now. The demise of my periods birthed in me a keen desire to seek out "Mother Nurture" on a fairly regular basis. If I go too long without reaching out and touching someone or something that brings me joy, my moods take a nosedive.

Is it working?

Let's just put it this way. It's been a long time since I've had a craving for a 9 x 13 pan of lasagna.

● ● ● ● ● ● ● **MENTAL-PAUSE:** ● ● ● ● ● ● ●

Reach *Out* to Heal What's Within

Touch. Think about it. It's something we do nearly every time we move our hands. We usually touch something or someone without giving it a single thought.

But touch is a nurturing healer, and not just for the person who's receiving it; maybe more so for the person who's giving it.

I remember, years ago, reading a little book written in the mid-80s called *Healed of Cancer* by Dodie Osteen. (Dodie just happens to be the mother of Joel Osteen, the pastor who wrote the mega bestseller *Your Best Life Now: 7 Steps to Living at Your Full Potential.*)

Dodie had been diagnosed with an extremely aggressive liver cancer and was given just months to live. How did she handle it? She visited the sick in her husband's church. (He, too, was a pastor, founding America's now largest congregation with more than 30,000 members, Lakewood Church in Houston, Texas.)

Dodie touched them, nurtured them, prayed for them, and babied them with motherly kindness. They were her alyssum, and she was determined to help them grow.

Even when she felt her worst, she got out of bed, put on a dress (she was into wearing dresses on a daily basis back then), and reached out to others. I don't know about all the people Dodie touched, but at the writing of this book the woman is still alive today, sitting regularly in her son's enormous congregation.

Then there's a friend who recently lost her husband of some 25 years. She is a smart, savvy businesswoman who could have tried to escape the grief by immersing herself in her work. But do you know what she did? Just days after she laid her husband to rest, she went out and bought a puppy—something she could cuddle and something that would cuddle her back.

My mother has found that cooking hordes of food (when she's only 90 pounds and eats like a bird) feeds her own need to nurture. The goodies sit lovingly in her freezer so that whenever one of her kids or grandkids come by, she has something to send home with them. Rightfully so, she's earned the loving nickname of "Meals on Wheels" in our family.

How long has it been since you intentionally touched, nurtured, and mothered someone or something simply to make them—or it—bloom into something better? How long has it been since you exercised your innate maternalness and babied someone or something? And just as important: How long has it been since YOU have babied YOURSELF? How long has it been since you've had a soothing surge of oxytocin in YOUR body?

My husband and I are keenly aware of when we're both having touch withdrawal. (Yes, men need it too, and it's perhaps one of the easiest ways to keep the feelings of an aging marriage soft and youthful.) There is a drafty coldness and hardness that shows itself in the way we talk and relate to one another, and it is now not uncommon for one of us to say to the other "I need to be touched" when we feel ourselves getting to that point. A conscious effort on the part of the other is all it takes for softness and kindness to once again grow in our relationship.

Look around you, sister. Fields of alyssum are just waiting for your touch to make them bloom.

Shopping for Love

Whether 16 or 60, mating and dating issues are no less daunting.

● ● ● ● ● ● ● ● **POWER SURGES** ● ● ● ● ● ● ● ●

The hunger for love is much more
difficult to remove than the hunger for bread.

MOTHER TERESA

The fruit of the Spirit is love, joy, peace, patience, kindness,
goodness, faithfulness, gentleness and self-control. Against such
things there is no law. Those who belong to Christ Jesus have
crucified the sinful nature with its passions and desires. Since
we live by the Spirit, let us keep in step with the Spirit.

GALATIANS 5:22-25

I slipped the little gift bag over her doorknob, thankful she wasn't home. For once I'd rather let a present do the talking for me.

I checked its contents one last time and grinned. I tried to imagine my friend's face, one that had seen too many tears these days, when she peeked inside and found three pair of lacy, frilly, teensy-weensy underwear she'd probably never dare to buy for herself.

Smiling, I read the gift card I'd written yet again. "God cares about even the smallest, most intimate details of your life." I said a quick prayer and drove off, hoping my off-the-wall present to a girlfriend whose husband of 35 years had just up and left her for another woman would hit its mark.

It's a target I've had some practice aiming at lately as my husband and I have seen far too many long-term marriages, both Christian and non, end as a result of divorce or death. But this one took us all by surprise. Especially Diana. She'd had no idea her husband had been shopping for a newer model until the day that he packed his bags and left.

It was that shopping trip of his that I wanted to address. I knew the devastation of her husband's behavior, and I so wanted to someday share it with Diana. "This is not about you, Di," I very much wanted to assure her. And the tiny undies were my way of doing so. I knew that her entire identity as a woman of value had been assaulted by a person she'd trusted. I understood.

You see, among other things I'm a recovered shopper myself. I was a teen in the '60s when the term "free love" surfaced in American vernacular at a terrible cost. I fell for it. Lock, stock, and barrel. And I paid an enormous price for something that was anything but free.

I was pretty much the consummate consumer, jumping from boyfriend to boyfriend by the time I met a guy I thought was marriage material. Without too much thought I said yes to his engagement proposal. I mean, that's what young girls did back then, right?

What on earth was I thinking?

I can ask that question of myself now, because some 35 years later, I realize I simply wasn't. Thinking, that is.

Those were the days way before premarital counseling became a prerequisite in most churches, and there was no one in my life with guts enough to ask the probing questions I've now asked the two of my four children who have so far married. Questions like: Why are you getting married? Does this person make your heart pound? What are his or her weaknesses? What are their strengths? How do they view key marital issues like sex and money? And the quintessential biggies:

Do you believe before God that this is the spouse He's prepared for you? Does he/she feel the same way about you?

But back to that random decision (and I stress the word "random") I made so many years ago. Let me make myself perfectly clear here. There was absolutely nothing wrong with the guy I wound up marrying, but there was a whole lot wrong with me. And it goes back to that shopping business. Even though I got a perfectly decent guy, I simply couldn't stop the addictive window-shopping.

Within just a few years I was in a full-blown extramarital affair with an equally married man who came packing his own shopping list.

We split from our spouses, leaving in our wakes two devastated people who must have questioned every aspect of their identity. Whether or not they were valuable. Desirable. Lovable. We got divorced and moved in together. Great way to start a relationship, huh? Two adulterers living together. Not a very firm foundation to build upon, is it? And then something great happened. Our house burned to the ground and we lost absolutely everything.

I remember standing in the driveway weeping over the dying embers and realizing that I didn't own a toothbrush. I didn't even own a single pair of panties other than the pair that was on my sorry behind. And yet I would soon come to find out that it was the best thing that could have happened to me. I would also come to the opinion that most everyone should—at least once in their life and painful as it may be—feel as though they have lost everything they have.

See, when you've lost everything, you no longer have anything to lose. I looked at my decimated life and thought that the status quo was simply not working for me. And so within a few short weeks I made 1) a drastic decision to depart from my shopaholic ways and 2) a deal with God.

I moved in with my brother and his wife, who were both Christians, and began to read the Bible. A particular passage, Acts 2:38, captured my attention. "Repent and be baptized, every one of you, in the name of Jesus Christ for the forgiveness of your sins. And you will receive the gift of the Holy Spirit." *I can do that,* I said to myself.

I'd read enough of the Book by this time to know that the Holy Spirit was described as "Counselor" and "Comforter." And I knew I wanted counsel and comfort. I wanted that more than I wanted any future shopping trips.

"Okay, okay, okay," I said one evening in the darkened room my brother was letting me stay in. "I'll do this repentin' thing, God. And I'll get baptized too." I determined I'd do the real-deal repenting, meaning I'd change my ways. No more man-land shopping trips. Abstinence, honesty, and morality would be my personal plumb line for behavior. Or at least that would be the target I'd aim for. But I added a caveat to the clouds: "If You really *are* up there, God, You've got 30 days to prove it to me. Otherwise, I'm goin' shoppin' for a bigger, better god." I flushed my birth control pills down the toilet. But, so doubtful was I that God even existed, I kept the prescription. I mean, I might have been desperate, but I wasn't stupid.

Suffice it to say that within 30 seconds of me being baptized in the ice-cold Spokane River in Spokane, Washington, on March 31, 1976, God arrived! He flat showed up! How do I know? Because when I walked out of that river I felt something different than I'd ever felt in my life. I felt clean. Forgiven. Holy and, for the first time in a long time, hopeful. Shopping trips now felt like heresy. At the very core of my being, I deeply sensed Someone—an entity that I didn't yet know or understand—had His arms around my heart and was loving me in a way that was so profound it still moves me to tears today.

While I wouldn't call it such until 30 years later, the *"I love you, Daughter. You're forgiven"* that I heard resounding throughout my being was the ultimate Hot Flash from Heaven. The fiery holiness of it has sustained me—and my monogamy—for more than three decades now.

The adulterous, by now ex-boyfriend heard about my experience in those waters and it must have given rise to some of his own soul searching. He was baptized a short time later. Weeks (that felt like years) of challenging abstinence went by when we both learned that God was enough to sustain our singleness.

Finally, we decided we needed to do the right thing—in the right chronological order. We married on May 21, 1976, and within about three months were pregnant with our first child, who was born the following May. In 2006 we celebrated our thirtieth wedding anniversary, demonstrating that there is hope for even the most hopeless of shopaholics.

Which returns us to Diana and the dilemmas that inevitably face the newly single, even in midlife. Maybe especially in midlife. And especially in our try-before-you-buy society today. Whether by way of death or divorce, abrupt singleness sometimes catapults otherwise sensibly mature women into insane shopping frenzies to prove their own worth. Women like Sadie.

She was a bright, beautiful, middle-aged Christian woman whose double-decade-long marriage turned into a train wreck when she found out her globe-trotting husband had another family in an entirely different country. Now, that wasn't Sadie's fault. And neither was the divorce that resulted from it. But the choices she made after it were, well, let's just say more consumerlike than Christian.

Rightfully, Sadie was more than freaked out at the idea of trusting any man ever again. And also rightfully so, she felt enormously unvalued and unattractive as a result of her husband's rejection. So she did what seems so acceptable in our society today—something that I worried would eventually be Diana's temptation as well.

She began to try a few men on for size, so to speak, and gave away far too much of her heart, and her body, in the process.

Her countenance—the innocence on her face, a reflection of her heart—tarnished. She had a hard time holding her head up around friends; and as a result, she lost some of them in the process. She didn't go to church for quite some time. Not that I think that's a prerequisite for closeness with God, but her reluctance to socialize with anyone on a spiritual level was an indication that all was not right with her soul. And while she claimed she still felt close to God, the lack of peace on her face didn't demonstrate it. The shopaholic men she met devalued her as soon as they found out she was "marked down and on the bargain table at a reduced price."

A common quote in my mother's growing up years still holds water today: "Why buy the cow when the milk is free?" That is so, so true. No wonder today's single women—no matter what their age—often wind up crying over the spilt milk of their intimate lives.

I remember debating this point with a dear older friend of mine some 20 years ago. She, too, had lost a husband; only it was to another kind of infidelity. His mistress was alcohol. And she, too, had valid reasons for the painful divorce she was finally forced to initiate in midlife.

But it was how she chose to soothe that pain that had troubled me. And I was close enough to her to tell her so. She was in her fifties back then, and I'm sure I came off as a know-it-all 35-year-old. In fact, she said almost exactly those same words to me after I'd told her I was troubled by her sleeping with men to try to heal the ache in her heart over her own losses.

"Just wait until you're my age," she said, "and we'll see how you view things then." It wasn't as argumentative an interchange as you would think. We were—and still are—both strong-willed women not afraid to voice our opinions or hear those of others.

And that returns me to today—the day I'm fleshing out this chapter. I am now exactly the same age my friend was when she made that little prognostication about my change of opinions and behaviors once I was in menopause (or in her case, the more proper spelling might have been men-no-pause). That day is now here. And I haven't changed my opinions in the least. But *she* has.

This woman is now in her mid-seventies and we are still good friends. Good enough for her to have long forgotten how she'd predicted I would think once I hit midlife quandaries like the loss of a spouse and the excruciation of shopping for a new one. The irony is that now she has a soapbox much larger than my own: One born by personal experience.

"How do these women today get off thinking it's okay to sleep around and that they have to try all these guys out?" she sermonized to me recently. "I think there's a reason God put things in chronological order: courtship, engagement, marriage, sexual intimacy."

I smiled at her as I enjoyed seeing one of those full-circle moments that aging sometimes allows us to savor. It wasn't worth it to me to remind her that she was now preaching to the choir and that she hadn't always felt, or acted, that way. It was joy enough to see her reflecting on life with changed perspectives.

Boy, did I want to tell Diana that. And not just Di, but all the rest of my middle-aged girlfriends whose marriages have vaporized as a result of divorce or death. And that includes Mary. A woman whose spouse passed away unexpectedly at the tender age of 62. Mary had ridden on her husband's spiritual coattails nearly all her life. She dutifully followed him to church, but it was clear that it was Herb who had the vibrant relationship with a Savior.

When Herb passed away, Mary was lost. Less than a month after he was gone, she called me late in the evening, terribly lonely on her sprawling ranch. "I can't live here without a man," she wept. While I tried to comfort her, it wasn't many weeks before she began shopping. On the Internet. And she met a man who was more than happy to take advantage of her loneliness—and her willingness to compromise values she had never really cultivated in the first place. He moved in with her in short order. Several years later, Mary's life is still in turmoil trying to build an on-again, off-again relationship with him on shifting sand.

I didn't want any of this for Diana. I knew, more than most, where shopping trips can lead. The day I left that little gift on her doorknob I was aiming for the mark in her heart that all of us have. The place that desperately needs to know that God can be enough in times of loss. In times of singleness. And that He really does care about all the intimate details of our lives.

And then I wondered. When will that time come for me? For my husband? When one of us dies before the other? And how will either of us tackle that temptation to once again go shopping? It's my prayer that the same determination that sustained us when we were brand-new Christians at the separate ages of 25 and 30 will resurface decades later. That God will target our hearts, once again, with His crystal clear message that He is more than enough.

● ● ● ● ● ● ●   **MENTAL-PAUSE:**   ● ● ● ● ● ● ●

Rethinking the Dating Game

For a refreshing argument against the twenty-first century's concept of what I call "serial dating," read Rob Eagar's book *Dating with Pure Passion*. The principle espoused in the book is an ageless one: That never before in history have we as a culture treated male-female courting with such a serious lack of societal guidelines or respect.

As a correspondent for my local newspaper, I remember doing a story on a young couple whose marriage I'd recently witnessed. When the groom took the bride's hand to walk up to the altar, it was the first time he had held her hand. The couple had long before made some rules for their courtship—no physical contact that would tempt them to compromise their dedication to abstinence before marriage, and no being completely alone together for long periods of time. When they dated, they usually dated in the safety of groups.

At the wedding, when the pastor pronounced, "You may now kiss the bride," it was the couple's very first kiss—and it was a scorcher. You could have ignited a nuclear power plant with the passion in that first kiss that we, as an audience, were privileged to witness.

Ten years later the couple has a beautiful family of three lovely little girls and talks frequently to schools, churches, and even radio programs about their unorthodox approach to shopping, I mean dating.

Does that mean that thumbing their noses at try-before-you-buy dating and frenzied shopping trips trying to find the "right one" guarantees that their relationship will always have smooth sailing? No. That they'll never lose their spouse? Certainly not.

But my expectation is that the purity with which they started adulthood will likely guide them should they once again find themselves single. I'm betting that they will cling to the knowledge that God is enough. He's enough companionship. He's enough comfort. Married or not. Single or not. Widowed or not.

May this same knowledge be mine and yours and gals like Diana, if, and when, we all have to walk through midlife and beyond without a spouse.

Letters to the Past

Gut-punching the grip of guilt.

He who cannot forgive breaks the bridge over
which he himself must pass.

GEORGE HERBERT

When you stand praying, if you hold anything
against anyone, forgive him, so that your Father
in heaven may forgive you your sins.

MARK 11:25

I knew what needed to be said. I'd had plenty of time to think about it. More than a quarter of a century, in fact. And yet the words hung in the air like a hangman's noose. This would either be one of the stupidest things I'd ever done or one of the smartest. But I knew, either way, that I simply had to do it. Such is the driving force behind midlife missions like these.

I could have written these letters anytime after that day in 1976 when I decided to give God a chance in my life. Little did I know at that time that it was I who was being given the chance. The chance to change.

And change I did. So much so that I knew that the three letters waiting to be written on my desktop that day had been waiting for far, far too long.

I started with the toughest and most important one first.

"Dear Mike..."

Strange as it might sound, I was writing a letter of apology to an ex-husband I'd cheated on more than three decades before. An ex who did nothing to deserve what I had done to him. If you've read this far in my book, you already know the story of my life BC (Before Christ...or...Before Change, whichever you prefer. For me, they're synonymous).

You've read how I did it ("it" is called adultery, if you haven't gotten that one by now), who I did it with (a fellow adulterer who would eventually make his own decision to also change), and what the outcome was (a transformed life of 30 years of monogamous marriage for the two of us "recovered adulterers," which now includes four grown children and their assorted wonderful mates and families). So no need to go back into that sordid tale of mudhole-turned-oasis again.

The story here is why I was writing to my ex, a person I had only bumped into (despite the fact that we lived in the same town) twice in all those years since. Plain and simple, it needed to be done. He deserved it.

Midlife gives many women (and, I suppose, men too) this type of perspective. From the back of our conscience it whispers that haunting things from the past need to be made right before we leave this planet, and that sometimes the only way to gut-punch the grip of guilt about the past is to go back to it.

So there I headed. Back into the past. I was following the words of a Hot Flash from Heaven I'm sure many aging women get but few act on. It was a repeat of an old Nike tennis shoe ad. *"Just do it."*

And so that's what I was doing.

Sucking up my pride, I was following those instructions.

I'll admit that it felt strange to think of whom I was writing to. But the nudging assured me it was more than time, if not long overdue, to *"just do it."*

If that wasn't motivation enough, the knowledge of the Scripture found in Mark where Jesus instructed His followers regarding the power of forgiveness was. I hoped, with all my heart, that others had been reading that same Scripture.

I pictured my ex's face that had surely aged over the years. I envisioned the shock—maybe even hatred, anger, or bitterness—on it when he saw the return name on the envelope. But then I saw what I was praying would happen to him, and to me, as we simultaneously became freed of a burdensome burden that only the right words could fix.

The words? They had to come from me and me alone.

"It wasn't your fault."

"It was my fault. I take all the blame."

"You didn't do anything wrong."

And the most important of all, "I am so sorry. Will you forgive me?"

The last two sentences were the ones I most needed to write: The ones that seem hardest for us humans—whether young or old, male or female—to cough up. I'm guessing it's because they're perhaps the *second* most powerful words that can bring healing to equally broken hearts and relationships. (I'll tell you the *first* most powerful words in a minute.)

I expected absolutely no response after all these years. In fact, I even told him so in the letter. I wanted to spare him the awkwardness of responding to my apology. In fact, a reply from him wasn't even on my radar screen as a possibility. He owed me nothing. There was nothing left that could be said—or so I thought. Too much water under the bridge, as they say.

Nevertheless, I wrote the one-page letter that followed the first two words, "Dear Mike." My last words were those two sentences that most needed to be said: "I am so sorry. Will you forgive me?"

The next letter was easier—but in some ways even more emotional—to write. It was to his mother. I was now in *her* shoes. I am now the mother of sons much the same age as hers was when I entered and then exited his life and hers. I am also now a mother-in-law who, like that woman did for me so many years ago, loves her in-law children as if they were her own.

I thought to myself, *I am right where she was in life when she got the news that her daughter-in-law had cheated on her precious son.* So it was easy to put myself in those shoes. I knew just how this woman likely felt seeing her son hurt so badly. All I had to do was imagine one of my own children being wounded like that.

I would have felt it all. Rage. Betrayal. Brokenheartedness. For both my son *and* myself. And much, much second-guessing.

Was there something wrong with my child that had driven his spouse into the arms of someone else? Something *I* caused in his upbringing? Something his father caused? What happened? Was there anything I could have said or done to make a difference? Was there anything my son should have said or done?

All those questions would have likely riddled me with guilt, guilt, guilt, and more guilt. And I wanted to, once and for all, free her from that.

And so my words to her were much the same—and yet very different—than the ones to her son.

"You did absolutely nothing wrong," I wrote with maternal tears dripping onto the paper.

"Your son did nothing wrong."

"It was *my* sin, not his. And definitely not yours. You did a wonderful job of raising a fine boy who did his best to be a good man—and a good husband."

And last but not least: "I am so sorry. Will you forgive me?"

And I added something. Something that was truer than I would have ever imagined. "Now that I am a mother-in-law myself, I remember all the wonderful things you did for me and my former marriage, and I try to model myself after you."

Again, I never expected a response. She, too, owed me absolutely nothing.

Then there was the last letter. The most complex of all. The letter to my husband's ex.

Bill has never been a letter writer. And he likely wouldn't have known what to say—or how to say it—even if he was. Besides, this wasn't something he felt he needed to do.

This was all about me. About my part in something that must have hurt another woman tremendously that I wanted to make restitution for.

I wasn't writing the letter on behalf of my husband. That was his own business to deal with however he chose to deal with it. This particular apology was coming directly from me. Because she, too, needed to know what I'd known for decades; that she truly had done nothing wrong. It had never been her fault. And, again, I needed to say those words: "I am so sorry. Will you forgive me?"

I finished her letter just as I finished the others. Short and sweet. On one page that also included a single paragraph, in addition to my apology, that I wanted each of the three recipients to know: That I had changed. *We* had changed. My husband of numerous decades and I had both changed and we were holding firm to that change.

I didn't want to come off like some death row inmate justifying his right to live by the fact that "I've found Jesus," but I just had to say it. No one else deserved the credit for such a dramatic lifestyle change. And I hoped that the fact that the change had been so long-lasting might make my "I'm sorry" much more believable to three people who deserved the truth, the whole truth, and nothing but the truth.

That's something I've learned in midlife—at this place our fore-mothers so appropriately christened The Change of Life. The words "I am so sorry. Will you forgive me?" are completely empty without change.

Madison, an old friend of ours, learned the same lesson. And she demonstrated it, as I did, with a letter. A letter to a former member of her congregation that she'd deeply wounded years before. Unlike my actions so many years ago, her intentions had been good. She had merely gone to a fellow Christian "in love" to tell him of his sin—or what she thought was his sin. More than a decade later she would recant her words. She'd been wrong. Her hyper-spirituality had blinded her to the fact that her friend had been right. Her friend had been my husband.

"I am so sorry. Will you forgive me?" were the words that drenched my husband's heart like a healing rain as he wept over that letter. A letter he still keeps in his office desk to this day. He could tell that Madison had changed. That she was no longer the judgmental, overly zealous young Christian she'd once been. That she'd realized that with change the words "I am so sorry. Will you forgive me?" become the most potent medicine for inner healing there is. Except, that is, for two other words that I'll get to shortly.

With the lick of my three envelopes, the thing that had been troubling me for three decades was finally off my mind.

Or so I thought.

A few days later the phone rang. There was no mistaking the caller ID. I was stunned. Scared. And shaking in my boots. The last thing I'd expected was *that* name on my caller ID. My three letters had each included the same sentence: "You do not need to respond to this letter."

Nevertheless, here it was. A response. A response from Mike. And his very first two words were the ones that I've *now* learned are even more powerful than "I am so sorry. Will you forgive me?"

It had been at least 20 years since I'd last heard his voice, but there was no mistaking it or the gift it carried. His very first words to me? "You're forgiven."

He said the two words in a tone that was both kind and genuine. A tone, I'm sure, that was tempered by time and maturity and much, much grace and generosity.

Those two words brought me to tears. And so did the sentences that followed as he shared his heart about what life had been like for him for nearly ten years after I'd done what I'd done. Understandably, as a result of my actions, he'd had trouble trusting women. A lot of trouble. And it had worn on him deeply.

"I had pictured us with the white picket fence, the whole thing," he said, openly transparent. The depth of the emotion after all these years unnerved me almost as much as those first two words. But it was good for me to hear, and it reinforced what I already knew: Selfish acts on behalf of one individual can have far-reaching consequences for another. But he also shared with me his joy at finding a wife he *could* trust—a woman he now called his soul mate. And I was deeply happy—and relieved—for him.

We chatted for a few minutes more, exchanging updates on how many children and grandchildren we each had, what we each were doing in these more golden years, and then we wished the other well. It had a calming effect on me, like a wine that had finally aged to just the right taste. I sensed it had the same impact on him.

When we said goodbye, I think we both knew we would likely never speak again. But that's the way it can be when just a few heartfelt sentences are exchanged between the wounded, no matter how much water has passed under the bridge. "I am so sorry. Will you forgive me?" and "You're forgiven."

Nothing more needs to be said with an exchange like that: It's a verbal bridge from the painful past to present-day healing that restores peace to both parties.

● ● ● ● ● ● ● ● **MENTAL-PAUSE:** ● ● ● ● ● ● ● ●

Give Yourself a Gift and Forgive Before You're Asked

A few days after that conversation, a note arrived in the mail. I recognized her handwriting immediately.

Like mother, like son, I thought to myself as I peeled the small note card open. My brave, sweet, former mother-in-law, who was now in her late-seventies, had also responded.

Her words were measured—and treasured—as she, too, transparently reminisced about the pain that I'd caused her. I knew she wasn't trying to make me feel worse than I already did, but there's something else I've discovered about going back to the past.

Like real-life physical wounds, when emotional and relational wounds are created, they need to be acknowledged, not ignored, by those who've inflicted them. No matter how many years have gone by, time alone does NOT always heal all wounds. Sometimes injuries need tending in order to get to the point of mending.

In writing to her, I had given her the opportunity to lance that old wound and let pour out what would pour out. And she had done it, like her son, in thoughtful dignity and even kindness that passed on the far deeper message: "You're forgiven."

In case you're wondering, I never heard from my husband's ex. And for that I am profoundly grateful. That was perhaps the greatest kindness of all. I would not have wanted her to ever be placed in an awkward situation by me again. And that's, I'm sure, how it would have felt for her to write that kind of note or place that kind of phone call. Some injustices, once repented of, are best put to rest.

Which brings me to my question for you. Could you have done what my ex did so graciously? Could you say those two most powerful words in the world: "You're forgiven" the way he did? Somehow I doubt that he could have said those words so soon after my letter arrived had he not already reached that place in his heart.

So picture your own letter from someone from the past who deeply hurt you. Can you envision forgiveness? Can you mouth the words "You're forgiven" right now? Or are you still filled up with so much of that angst-filled antithesis to forgiveness, bitterness, that it would choke the words right out of you?

Yes, forgiveness is a gift for the recipient, but the greatest receiver of the gift is the giver of forgiveness.

Recent research at places as eminent as Harvard University indicate the incredibly powerful mental, emotional, and physical health benefits for the person who gives the forgiveness, even when it's not asked for. Depression can lift, blood pressure can drop, and a general feeling of wellness can replace gnawing emptiness.

You don't have to wait for repentance to grant forgiveness. If you don't believe me, go ask the One who went up on a cross for you a couple thousand years ago. For more on this subject go to the website www.forgiving.org and visit chapter 12 of this book.

Mother-in-Law from Paradise or Purgatory?

Which am I? Or do I have multiple personality disorder?

POWER SURGES

*Mother-in-law: A woman who destroys her son-in-law's
peace of mind by giving him a piece of hers.*

AUTHOR UNKNOWN

*For this reason a man will leave his father and mother and
be united to his wife, and the two will become one flesh.*

EPHESIANS 5:31

So *this is what you look like,* I thought to myself, as I surveyed the
sandy-blond, 22-year-old young man sitting tensely in our living
room. *You're not at all what I'd expected.* I always thought girls married men who looked and acted somewhat like their fathers. *Some sort
of Freudian thing,* I mused as my husband and I watched him fidget
nervously in his chair.

But this short, piercingly blue-eyed, slightly baby-faced young man
looked nothing like my much taller, brown-eyed, olive-skinned, burly

husband Bill. The kid's quick wit and even quicker smile were also a reminder of how different the two were in many ways, as Bill leaned toward the more serious side. The fact that the young man also was named William seemed to be about the only thing the two shared besides a love of two things: All endeavors hunting and fishing related and our only daughter, Libby. But even the boy's nickname was a hair different from my husband's. He was called Will by family and friends. The difference in his name would serve us well in coming years.

I'd been preparing myself for this day since the time, a couple of years ago, when I was talking with a girlfriend on the phone while multitasking online. As we gabbed I lightly perused my e-mail, stopping immediately at the one with my daughter's return address on it.

I loved hearing from Libby. Even though she was just a couple hours' drive south of us at the University of Idaho, we didn't get to see each other nearly as often as I would have liked.

As my girlfriend chattered on, I opened Libby's letter, thinking I could keep up my conversation with my friend while lightly scanning my computer screen.

But then I read the first two sentences in my daughter's lengthy e-mail. "Dear Mom: People say that you know when you've met 'the one' you're going to marry. Well, I think I've met 'the one.'"

Screech. Slam on the brakes. "Gotta call you back, girlfriend," I said into the phone. I slammed it down as if I'd just found out my pants were on fire. She'd understand my abruptness if this e-mail was going the direction it looked like it was from those first sentences. This was no time for doing two things at once. I had to read with undivided attention.

My daughter went on to describe this new guy in her life and what she liked about him: That he was the first boy/man (what are they really when they're just twenty-something and courting your daughter?) she'd ever met who took *her* to church instead of the other way around. Oh, and another apparently important thing to my daughter: "He makes me laugh even more than my brothers."

Then she cued me in on a few incidentals. "He'll probably never make much money, Mom. He wants to be a teacher. And, well, he's shorter and younger than me."

More screeching and slamming on the brakes. *Great,* I thought to myself. *Has my daughter just fallen for a 12-year-old still on an allowance?*

We'd find out within just a matter of weeks when Libby told me she was bringing Will home to meet us. One of those pesky Hot Flashes from Heaven struck quicker than a suitor hitting on my daughter.

"It's time to start treating the people your children date as if they are potential in-laws," it forewarned.

"Huff," grumped my husband when I tried to relay that little message from the heavens to him and told him to be on his best behavior with Will. If I'd simply told him this young man (who proved to be half an inch shorter and a half a year younger than our daughter) was just a friend of hers that she was on some college committee with, Bill would never have reacted that way. But the father had also read the daughter's e-mail, and he was already acting like a typical male dog with a fire hydrant way too close to him. Now, I mean that with no disrespect to my husband or his gender, but men tend to do weird things to—how do I put this delicately?—mark their territory.

And poor, unsuspecting Will Fridinger was venturing dangerously close to Bill Snyder's territory.

I wish I could tell you that my husband rose to the occasion when we finally met Will. But he didn't. He made a show of, well, "watering his fire hydrant." Staying a bit cool, a bit reserved with Will, he looked over the top of his reading glasses at the kid's desperate attempts to make polite conversation and milked it for all it was worth.

My husband has an enormous heart of gold and loves his kids deeply. At the same time, he can manifest a gruff exterior that sometimes makes a person tend to think otherwise. After years of enduring this enigma, I only had a couple things to say to the man after Will and Libby had left.

"Are you insane? How could you? Don't you realize this boy could someday be our son-in-law? And he will never, ever forget how you treated him. Do you want him to think you're a purgatorial father-in-law? If you love our daughter, then you WILL love the man she loves!"

Lesson number one on how to be the in-law from paradise or purgatory had just hit us, and I knew we both had tough choices to make.

All I got was another "huff" from the husband. But there. I'd spit out the sacredly scary words: "In-law."

Libby was, after all, the first of our four children to be on the threshold of this life-changing nomenclature. And my husband had only a short reply. "Well, he'll have to get past me first."

So there we sat, a couple years later, in our living room. Will had refused to be scared off by Bill, and Libby's young man was now on one side of the room with my husband on the other and me in the middle. *How very appropriate,* I thought, smirking internally. Bill had slowly warmed to the many great attributes the kid had. He was hardworking, driven, and goal oriented, and he cared about "God stuff." And, as our daughter had first noticed, he was funny enough to take on all three of her comedic brothers. And yet Bill still seemed determined to guard a fire hydrant or two. Oh, the power of the father-driven desire to protect his "womenfolk."

We both knew why Will was there. At first he'd tried to phony up a story that he wanted to come up to our place to take us out for lunch "just because." Yeah, right. No self-respecting, busy college guy wants to take his girlfriend's parents out for lunch "just because."

"Spit it out, Will," I had said to him over the phone as a reply to his lame "just because" invitation. By then I had a pretty relaxed, joke-bantering relationship with him that I had nurtured carefully. Thank goodness I'd heeded that Hot Flash a couple years back and, from the very get-go, treated him like the son-in-law he just might become. In other words, I exercised Lesson Number Two in how to be the mother-in-law from paradise. I tried my best to stay on his good side no matter what it cost me.

Fortunately that was not hard. He's a pretty easygoing guy. But I really worked the mothering angle—baking him cookies when he came for visits, having pleasantly long academic and spiritual discussions with him that gave me clues to the good my daughter saw in him, and focusing on loving the positive in him. As far as I knew it was working. I think he might even have decided he liked me.

"You don't have to buy us lunch to ask us what I think you've got up your sleeve," I asserted. "Cut to the chase, Son. What's this all about?"

"Well," he answered, carefully picking his words. "I'd like to ask for Bill's and your blessing for me to propose to Libby. She doesn't know anything about this. I'd like to ask her this weekend."

This weekend! It was two days away!

"Huff," growled Bill again when he heard the news. You'd have thought the man would have at least added a few more words to his vocabulary in the two years he had come to know the boy, er, man. No matter. Bill was still keeping his eye on his fire hydrants.

And then, the next day, there sat Will in our living room.

Which brings me back to what I was thinking as I watched him squirm in his chair like the kids he'd be teaching when he soon graduated.

So this is what you look like. I rolled that thought over and over in my mind.

You see, I'd been praying for this kid for 22 years now, ever since I'd learned I was pregnant with what might just become his prospective wife—our daughter, Libby.

And I thought back to all those years of prayer.

I was pregnant back in the days before ultrasounds were in vogue and new parents awaited the birth of their children clueless as to their sex. With each of my pregnancies, I had always prayed the same prayer in the same way. As soon as my suspicions were confirmed with a positive pregnancy test, I'd begin praying for that baby deep within my womb. That first of all they'd be born and grow up healthy and safe; but more important, that they'd mature into passionate God lovers. That their spirits would commingle with their Creator's and that they'd be transfused by His blood with a personality and joyful heart that chased after Him all the days of their lives.

And then I simultaneously prayed for another baby. The one that I believed God was probably already creating to be my child's mate. And I would pray the same thing for that little one, adding on the request that God would mold both these two unknown children—my own and someone else's—into eventual complements to each other.

Those prayers had remained regular and consistent throughout all the years since. And they often included deeper layers as I prayed for the grandchildren and great-grandchildren that would come from these unions and, yes, their spouses as well. I guess that makes me a generational pray-er. But I couldn't help it. I'm at peace with being an obsessive-compulsive prayer-mutterer.

I knew Will's history. His parents had divorced when he was young and his little heart was broken by it. I was praying for him then. They got back together when his mother found out she had cancer. I was praying for him then. His mom lost her battle with the disease when he was in his early teens, and he went into a freefall of emotions. I was praying for him then. He began acting out, rebelling against his dad, and he was angry and sad, as any teenager might be, given his level of grief. I was praying for him then. He headed off to college, where he did the stereotypical freshman frolics and darn near flunked out of school, even though he was brilliantly smart. I was praying for him then. He righted his course, and especially his relationship with his dad, with hard work and a newfound maturity. I was praying for him then. He began going to church, inviting my daughter in the process. Need I say more?

This optimistic, life-filled young man sitting terrified in our living room was the first fruit of all those years of prayers. As a result, I had a heart for him that went far deeper than he could have ever imagined at the time.

I know you, Will Fridinger, I thought to myself. *I've known you all your life.* I could barely hold back the flood of emotions. And yet my husband's deep baritone broke into my thoughts.

"I heard you have something to talk to us about, Will," he said with a deliberately stern mask over his face, looking every bit the part of the father-in-law from you-know-where. I'd been married to this Grizzly Adams-kinda guy for a long time now, and I could tell he was biting the inside of his cheek to keep from breaking out laughing. He was having far too much fun at the expense of poor Will.

"Well, I've…mmm…come…to…mmm…ask for your blessing to marry Libby."

Silence. My husband has refined the art of using it as a lethal weapon. I was used to it. Will was not. There was a bead of sweat beginning to form on Will's forehead. Still more silence.

Bill looked out the window with a faraway look in his eyes—as if he was contemplating beating the snot out of someone. *Oh, knock it off,* I wanted to tell my husband. *No one's going to give you an Academy award for this ridiculous performance.* But I knew this was a guy thing. A fire hydrant thing.

Finally, Will couldn't take the deafening silence any longer.

"I've already bought a ring," he said, fumbling in his pocket and pulling out a jeweler's box. He proudly popped it open to show he was dead serious about what he was doing. *He must be,* I thought to myself. *Dang! The kid bought my daughter a rock that is bigger than my own!* As a hardworking college student, I understood the ramifications of all that ring had cost him. My husband sized up the huge expense of the precious purchase and looked at it in an entirely different way. He was not about to release his daughter into the hands of a spendthrift.

"So tell me about your plans for the future, Will," Bill said, barely giving the stunning ring a sideways glance. He wasn't impressed by jewelry. He wanted to see the poor kid's stock portfolio.

As calmly as he could, Will laid out his goals, detailing his income working at a local grocery store while he finished his bachelor's degree, his desire to continue his education and get his master's after he and Libby were married, and his plans and passion to teach.

Then Bill turned to me. "Ronna, would you mind leaving the room and letting us talk?" I could see panic in Will's eyes. He would later tell us both that when I walked out of the room, he desperately wanted to ask my husband if he could just go with me. I went down the hall to our master bedroom and listened through the open door as I pretended I was making the bed. Even more silence.

Oh, Bill, for heaven's sake, give the kid a break, I wanted to yell back down the hall. But he had one last fire hydrant to attend to.

I couldn't hear my husband's hushed voice, but it would be later that day when Bill would tell me the Stradivarius story he'd told Will.

"Do you know what a Stradivarius is?" he had asked Will seemingly out of the clear blue sky. (The kid's IQ is off the charts. He'd surely know what his future father-in-law was about to lecture him on: That a Stradivarius is an extremely valuable violin made by the Italian master violin maker, Antonio Stradivari, in the late 1600s. There are only about 700 of the originals remaining in the world today, and a single original "Strad" is worth millions.)

"My daughter is a Stradivarius," my husband would explain to his captive audience of one. "Treat her like one and you can have my blessing. But if you don't," he paused for dramatic effect, "I'll hunt you down and whip your scrawny little behind."

This, I'm told by both my husband and now son-in-law, was the final icebreaker between the two. Such is frequently the case with that mysterious stuff called "man-talk." Go figure. Instead of flipping out at the fact that he might just have a homicidal father-in-law-to-be on his hands, Will's face broke into a huge, relief-filled smile. He looked at the body part he was sitting on and joked back, "Scrawny? Who're you callin' scrawny?"

The twosome's laughter rippled like fresh water down the hall to where I was standing as my husband hollered to me that the coast was clear. I could reenter the living room. I was relieved to find there weren't any dead bodies in it.

It was then that I finally got to officially slip into my mother-in-law shoes, the ones I'd practiced walking in for two years now. And, despite my heart for Will, I had a lecture or two up my sleeve as well.

Actually, they weren't so much lectures as requests. That's probably Lesson Number Three in opting to be the mother-in-law from paradise. Politely request. Try not to lecture.

At any rate, I had three conditions before I gave my full blessing on Will's proposal plans: 1) That he promise us that he and Libby would see a trained, master's level, premarital Christian counselor (I said that because oftentimes couples wind up getting premarital counseling from someone who might be a terrific pastor but not such a terrific counselor), 2) that they both read two books: *How to Have an Elegant Wedding for $5,000 or Less* by Jan Wilson and Beth Wilson Hickman and *Saving your Marriage Before It Starts: Seven Questions to Ask Before—and After—You Marry* by Leslie and Les Parrott III, and 3) that he'd be responsible to keep God number one in the couple's marriage. Will, relieved that he was no longer in the hot seat with Bill, eagerly agreed and the deal was done.

The next day, Easter Sunday, Will returned with Libby and her college friends for breakfast and a traditional egg hunt that my grown kids still insisted I do. With her dad videotaping the hunt, Libby found the last plastic egg—one that was significantly larger than all the rest. She looked questioningly around at her family and friends who were, by now, all watching as she opened it and saw the box inside. Her mouth dropped open in shock. Will then gently took it out of her hands and, in the same room that the day before he'd verbally dueled with Bill, got down on one knee and proposed to our speechless daughter.

I couldn't help noticing, as I saw my husband's smiling face behind the camera, that there was a lot more room for Will's bended-knee proposal in that crowded living room than there had been the day before. All the fire hydrants were finally gone.

● ● ● ● ● ● ● MENTAL-PAUSE: ● ● ● ● ● ● ● ●

Getting Territorial Yourself? Tame Thyself

Over the years I've learned much about being the mother-in-law from paradise, both from my married kids and from my own mother, a woman my husband calls "The Greatest Mother-in-Law in the World" largely because:

1. He knows there isn't a thing she wouldn't do for us if we needed her.

2. She loves our children wildly and, therefore, is a fabulous grandmother and great-grandmother.

3. She's never been territorial, keeps her nose out of our personal matters, and refuses to take sides.

4. She makes the best cheese rolls in the entire world.

My most challenging choice to date that I have had to make about which mother-in-law I would become was when one of my sons and his beautiful fiancée had an argument that I was partly drawn into.

I'd inadvertently made a comment that had hurt and angered the woman who would soon be my adored daughter-in-law. My son got caught in the crossfire.

I'll be perfectly honest here—and it is ugly. My first thought upon learning that the fiancée thought I'd breached a mother-in-law boundary was a seething, "I'll show her. She's gonna lose if she tries to come between me and my son because NO ONE will turn my son away from me."

Once I heard those internal words tempting my temper, I turned to the Scripture in Ephesians exhorting all spouses to cling to one another. Convicted and enormously shocked and ashamed at my untamed territorialism, I immediately called my son, who indeed felt caught in the middle, and told him, "No matter if I am right and she is dead wrong, you MUST learn to stand by HER side and not MINE. You absolutely MUST leave behind your parents' edicts and cleave to your wife, Son. And God, I promise you, will bless you for it."

So upon quizzing my family, here's a little checklist to keep in mind when you're making a choice as to whether or not your in-law actions go the way of paradise or purgatory.

A mother-in-law from purgatory:

- Often stays as territorial as a pit bull when it comes to letting go of her own child and embracing a new one.

- Lets her vices or addictions impact her child's new family. (I found this out when my now-deceased mother-in-law would call us late at night after drinking too much. It made my husband and me very sad and very angry.)

- Is overly possessive or, on the flip side, oblivious to her grandchildren, or she uses them as pawns to manipulate the parents; or even worse, she tells the parents how to parent.

- Puts undue pressure on her children when it comes time for holidays, weekends, etc., and where they'll spend those days—with the husband's or the wife's family.

- Is easily threatened by the couple's desire to forge new family traditions within their own household. The mother-in-law-from-purgatory's MO (method of operation) will be to use guilt to induce extended family time.

- Spends too little or, worse yet, too much time with the couple. (She wouldn't dream of asking the couple what works best for them.)

- Blows through boundaries, unconcerned if she has offended her in-law and makes life twice as difficult for her own child.

- Keeps a record of wrongs (who did what to whom in their in-law arguments).

- Tries to sabotage the couple's marital relationship.

- Prays "about" her in-law (complaining to God as if their child's betrothed is her adversary).

- Talks more than she listens.

A mother-in-law from paradise:

- Doesn't even think in terms of territory. She fully relinquishes control over her engaged or married children and allows them to be what they now are: Grown adults whose first priority must be to their own marriages and spouses.

- Deeply loves her children's children; but she keeps in mind that they are just that—her children's children and doesn't try to tell her in-law how to parent.

- Treats, loves, and views her new in-law as "family," even when the person might not temporarily deserve it or look like it; but simply because her OWN child loves this other person.

- Holds her child's new family with "open hands," recognizing that she will have to share her child with the in-law's family on holidays, etc.

- Continues to, for the sake of her own child, act as though she really, truly "likes" the in-law, even when she might temporarily be tempted to not.

- Keeps her criticisms to herself.

- Has gentle boundaries as to what she will and will not do as an in-law and respects the boundaries of the couple as well.

- Keeps no record of wrongs, realizing that couples disagree and then get over it and so she needs to also.

- Continues to encourage and support the couple's marital relationship.

- Prays "for" her in-law (as opposed to "about") as a loving teammate and family member committed to supporting their marriage.

- Listens more than she talks.

When the Cart Comes Before the Horse

Pregnant with joy—no matter how
you arrive in Grandma-land.

When a child is born, so are grandmothers.

JUDITH LEVY

*You created my inmost being; you knit me together
in my mother's womb. I praise you because I am fearfully
and wonderfully made; your works are wonderful, I know
that full well. My frame was not hidden from you when
I was made in the secret place. When I was woven together
in the depths of the earth, your eyes saw my unformed body.
All the days ordained for me were written in your book
before one of them came to be.*

PSALM 139:13-16

It had been a busy day of appointments and running errands in town, and I was late getting home that early May evening. I was tired and more than a little worn out by the ups and downs of menopausal hot flashes and insomnia that were causing me to guard how much I physically expended myself each day. Nevertheless, one of spring's first sun-drenched days in the Pacific Northwest beckoned me with its rosy-hued reminder that I still had many things to celebrate besides the sunshine.

I was just finishing a year-long ladies' Bible study commitment, which had involved a biweekly, two-hour round-trip into town. But it had been worth it. Over the year I'd gotten to better know the mostly middle-aged female church leaders in my group, and we'd shared many intimate parts of our lives as we'd cried, commiserated, and chuckled over the challenges that life presents us during The Change and its powerful precursor, perimenopause.

When the only youngster of our group, a lovely single 24-year-old we "meno-moms" all unofficially adopted as our daughter, got the cart before the horse and wound up pregnant out of wedlock, we rallied around her like the perfect Christian mothers we'd always longed to be.

In the process of encouraging her, several members of the group divulged that they'd either started their own parenting years in the same way or had children who had. Their successful marriages were a comforting confirmation to me that even when life implodes, God follows behind to resurrect the carnage and re-creates something beautiful out of it.

Following my girlfriends' example, I, too, put my arms around our pregnant little sister and said the one word the older ones had all confessed they'd so desperately wanted to hear when in the same predicament. "Congratulations."

But inwardly I sighed with relief and thankfulness that not only had I personally avoided the 24-year-old's fate so many years ago, but my only daughter was now married and, to the best of my knowledge, none of my three sons had serious girlfriends. I confess I felt that I was, just maybe, immune from having to worry about things like the chronological order of things like carts, horses, and premarital pregnancies. I guess you could say I was still hanging on to the last vestiges of midlife's maternal denial.

Despite a twinge of smugness that tempted me to believe that my incredible good fortune might somehow be due to my excellent mothering abilities, the stark realities of my friends' confessions had brought me back to earth. I have to admit that up until this time, I still thought I might just have been a good enough mom, a strong enough Christian, and an inspiring enough woman so that these kinds of challenges would never rear their heads in my life or the lives of my kids. It was a wonderfully, deliciously, unburst bubble.

I pictured my husband already at home from his day's work, settled back into his favorite chair to watch the evening news, and I knew he'd be wondering why I wasn't home yet to start dinner. I called him on my cell phone. "I'm on my way," I assured him. "Just one more stop to make."

Actually, there were two, but I didn't want to bore him with the details. And that last stop wouldn't take but a minute. Nor did I want to have to explain to him how very led I felt to make it.

I dropped off some mail at the rural post office, my next-to-last stop, and then I followed an internal prodding I simply couldn't shake. I detoured a block off the country road, parked my car in an obscure weed patch, and made my way into bushes behind an abandoned building. I knew just what I was looking for.

Nearby Spokane doesn't call itself the Lilac City for nothing. And the month of May heralds a literal eruption in our area of the fragrant lavender blooms that are some of my favorite flowers. At least once each year I make a roadside pit stop for the blossoms that grow wild along country roads, and I pick myself an extravagant bouquet, letting the perfume fill my car on the way home.

So there I was, knee deep in weeds and soon-to-be-fleeting fantasies. I was hidden from view behind the building, filling my arms with lilacs and reveling at the moment in the relative uncomplicatedness of my usually hormonally rocky life.

I heard the car long before it actually stopped. Its loud exhaust, which made me think it might be a fellow Harley rider, piqued my curiosity. I peeked around the bush to see if it was. It was anything but. It was my 23-year-old son, Simeon, in his noisy Nissan with the loud muffler—some 20 miles from his home in the city.

"I can't believe this. I can't believe I just saw your car here off the road," he said with an enormously sheepish grin as he unfolded his 6'5" frame out of the little car. We both marveled at the orchestrated coincidence that we'd wound up on the same out-of-the-way side road at the same out-of-the-ordinary time of day.

"I was at your house and I saw that Dad's car was there, but yours wasn't, so I didn't pull in. I wanted to talk to you first. I just had my hand on my cell phone and I was dialing to call you," Simeon continued, showing me the cell phone he still had tucked in his hand. He boosted himself up onto the hood of his car as if he was in no big hurry, his gangly legs hanging over the side. "I have something to tell you."

I stood there cradling the lilacs as he began to speak, now wondering if the leading I'd felt wasn't as much about picking lilacs as it was about being available at this exact moment. In this exact location. With this exact son.

"I haven't been too happy about where my life's been going. I haven't prayed in over a year," confided Simeon who, like many young men his age, had been placing parties far higher than prayer in his personal priorities.

"So I got down on my knees and prayed. I told God I wasn't even sure if He existed. And that if He did, I needed Him to let me know." By this time, Simeon's eyes had begun to mist over, and I saw a softness and vulnerability I hadn't seen on his face in a long, long time. He added quietly, "Unbeknownst to me, Sarah was doing the same thing on the same night at her place."

Sarah was a girl I'd met only once just recently, and yet I'd sensed she was special as she was the only girl my second son had ever asked to bring to our home for dinner. She was a pretty young woman—as tiny as my son was tall—with a gentle spirit and an even gentler voice. Like my son, she loved children and wanted to be a teacher.

"The next day," Simeon went on, "my boss told me I was getting a raise—a nice one; and I felt like things were, well, maybe different with God."

I smiled, not at the idea of the raise, but at what it represented: My son on his knees getting answers from God.

"And then the following day, Sarah was told that she just got one hundred percent health insurance benefits." That also brought a smile to my soul. I didn't really know Sarah, but any girl who'd get on her knees before God already had my heart.

"And then, the day after that," Simeon paused. He looked deeply into my eyes with tears now streaking down his face and flowing into a heartwarming smile. "We found out that Sarah's pregnant. You're going to be a grandmother."

Time stopped. And so did my heart. The earth quit rotating. Silence roared. Except for the sound of some imaginary horse I heard whinnying off in the distance: A horse that was coming well before the cart it should have been pulling. And bubbles were bursting like hydrogen bombs in my life. Bubbles that had deluded me into still believing that striving at being the perfect mother would somehow inoculate me, and my kids, against moments like this.

For one of the very first times in my articulate life, I was completely and utterly speechless. I was right where God often puts mothers like me: Quiet enough to hear a Hot Flash from Heaven that was as tiny, yet life filled, as a baby's first heartbeat.

"Like it or not, Daughter, I AM the God of Burst Bubbles. And I am STILL on the throne when kids get carts before horses," it said in lilac-fragranced love as I was, once again, face-to-face with that unavoidable fact The Change so aptly teaches us: We never DID have all the answers as parents. We just thought we did, or pretended we did, as we gullibly trudged on in motherhood, desperately holding on to the belief that if we just followed some holy formula everything would turn out perfectly in the final chapters of our lives and those of our kids'.

And now, like several of my girlfriends in the Bible study, the facetiousness of my own personal la-la-land was finally on my own doorstep, up close and personal, in the face of my son.

Simeon interrupted my silent thoughts. His beaming countenance reminded me of when he was seven years old and his cheeks would be flushed from pushing his baby brother around in a wagon—a pastime he'd so dearly loved that he still, despite his work as a custom home builder, longed to spend his days teaching kids. And now he'd have one of his own. Despite the seriousness of his circumstances, there was no denying the joy on his face. "And I am so freaked out and so excited at the very same time," he said through his glowing grin.

I was barely able to squeak out a reply. I needed silence, and lots of it, to take in all that I'd just been told. And I had the presence of mind to know I was no longer up to the task of sermonizing. So I cleared my throat and humbly uttered the only sage response I could muster.

"Welcome to parenthood, Son," I said. "Be prepared to feel like this for the rest of your life. Children, no matter how young or how old, will always have a particular knack for keeping parents so freaked out and so excited at the very same time." I thought about how those words so aptly described the eddy of emotions I was now floundering in.

Simeon babbled on about what a miracle it was that he was now making enough money that he'd be able to somehow support a baby—a responsibility Mr. Party would never have taken seriously three months ago. And that what an equal miracle it was that the pregnancy and birth would be fully paid for by Sarah's new insurance policy.

He shared that it had taken him three weeks to get up the courage to tell me. That he'd practiced by telling all his friends and even his siblings and that his dad and I were basically the last to know. He added that he'd wanted to tell his father and me separately (probably to let us each feel our own reactions in a "divide and conquer" strategy), and that he'd be telling his dad in the next few days.

Oddly, I was thankful for that. I didn't want the burden of having to debrief all of this with his father right now. I needed time to myself. Time to process that enormous, life-changing sentence I'd just heard: "You're going to be a grandmother."

Then he asked, would I please do one more thing in addition to not telling his dad until he had told him himself? I nodded my head tentatively. At that moment, I had absolutely no energy to deny the father of my first and only grandchild anything.

"Don't pressure us to get married yet," he said as politely but assertively as he could. He explained that he and Sarah needed time to adjust to the pregnancy without any added pressure.

I swallowed hard and blindly nodded yes, but it wasn't easy. A part of me wanted to exclaim, "Are you crazy? You put me in this position and you expect me to hold my tongue?" But no words, well intentioned or otherwise, would come. My mind was completely undone by that sentence I kept hearing over and over: "You're going to be a grandmother."

A grandmother. A grandchild. My husband, a grandfather. My son, a father.

And then I thought about the psalm we'd read to comfort the young pregnant woman in our Bible study: "You created my inmost being; you knit me together in my mother's womb. I praise you because I am fearfully and wonderfully made; your works are wonderful, I know that full well. My frame was not hidden from you when I was made in the secret place. When I was woven together in the depths of the earth, your eyes saw my unformed body. All the days ordained for me were written in your book before one of them came to be" (Psalm 139:13-16).

Tears filled my eyes as the sweet reality of those simple words overpowered my deep maternal drive to "fix" my child's, and now my grandchild's, life. As it did, it bathed my fears, my disappointment, maybe even my shame, and definitely that cart before the horse and those very burst bubbles, in calmness. The thought that, somehow, God would work this out and that no grandchild of mine could possibly be a "mistake" or "illegitimate"—no matter how, or when, he was conceived—filled me with a peace I'd never thought I'd have under the circumstances; a peace given to me by a God so personal that He'd patiently prepared me for this moment the entire past year.

Then I thought about the babe-in-the-womb I'd yet to meet: That little person I'd been praying for since Simeon himself had been in my own uterus. As I'd done with his sister and brother before him—and his little brother after him, I'd stayed steadfast in praying for not just their mates, but also their children and their children's children—faceless individuals and souls who were my very heart. My heritage. My legacy.

I'd prayerfully clung to Psalm 128:6 where the writer had prayed his own blessing on all believers when he wrote, "May you live to see your children's children." I had always wanted that: To live to see my children's children. And now here I was. Less than seven months away from that very day. How could I *not* thank God for an answered prayer simply because it didn't fit into my Plan A expectations for my life or my child's?

True, this wasn't at all how I'd pictured my first grandchild entering the world. But any disappointment I was tempted to feel was overshadowed by a resounding voice of reassurance, *"If I'm the God of burst bubbles and carts-before-horses, I'm also the God of Plan B."*

Plan B. Maybe it wasn't *my* version of the perfect plan, but it *was* a plan nonetheless. A plan that God could certainly perfect. A plan for my husband, for me, for our grandchild, for my son, and for Sarah that might surely fit into the framework of the verse in the Bible's book of Jeremiah that says, " 'For I know the plans I have for you,' declares the LORD, 'plans to prosper you and not to harm you, plans to give you hope and a future'" (Jeremiah 29:11).

Somehow, even if it would take all the strength I had, I decided I would trust in that. I would allow God to impregnate me with joy over this grandchild. And I would savor this first delicious step into grandmotherhood.

Then I thought once again of the 24-year-old in the Bible study. About how vulnerable she'd been. How frightened. How much reassurance she'd needed from us, her girlfriends. From her family. From her boyfriend. From her boyfriend's family. And my heart melted for Sarah—a woman whose last name I didn't even know, who was now, overnight, one of the most important people in my life. The mother of my first grandchild.

I looked down at all the lilacs in my hands as a smile spread across my own face. My bubble might have burst and my carts and horses might be in the wrong order temporarily, but God was still in control of Plan B, no matter how topsy-turvy my child's, and my own, answered prayers might look like at the moment.

"Here, Simeon," I said as I tenderly laid the enormous bouquet in his arms. "Give these flowers to Sarah for me and tell her, 'Congratulations.'"

●●●●●●● **MENTAL-PAUSE:** ●●●●●●●

Embracing The Change Often
Includes Embracing Plan B

How about you? Do you have a few carts before horses? Bubbles in need of bursting?

Or maybe your bubbles have already burst: An unmarried child winds up pregnant. A loved one unexpectedly dies far too young. A friendship fails. A marriage dissolves. Sometimes only God knows what misconceptions we've clung to that have tricked us into thinking that if we only DO everything perfectly, everything will BE perfect.

But if that were the case, we wouldn't need God, would we? All we'd need is our own self-righteous perfection. And then what a dismally imperfect relationship with a Savior we'd have.

The Change teaches us this sometimes better than any amount of prayer can. By virtue of our sheer mounting numbers of years upon the earth, we reap wisdom youthful naïveté often ignores.

We eventually see—despite all our best efforts and most fervent prayers—pregnant unmarried children, lost loved ones, failed friendships, and abandoned marriages.

If we still don't get it, books such as Dr. Larry Crabb's *Shattered Dreams: God's Unexpected Path to Joy* can further drive the point home.

I highly recommend reading these spiritually real writings if your bubble's burst or you've got catawampus carts and horses in your life.

I have to admit that there was a time when I couldn't read Crabb's writings. I joked that the well-known Christian psychologist and bestselling author, whose prayerfully pragmatic writings I now understand, was appropriately named Crabb for his cynical view of life.

But that was before The Big M hit. And my bubbles, one after another, burst. And wild horses—and even wilder children—kicked the sides right out of their carts. Then I, too, faced the unavoidable fact that life is literally riddled with burst bubbles and horses pushing, instead of pulling, carts. I finally laid down my denial and accepted the fact that within the popping of those false perspectives lies the true road to a faith so deep that it finally admits it needn't have all the answers. Just The Answer—a God who will always lead us to Plan B.

Speaking of Plan B—it included God urging me to quickly acknowledge how fearful Sarah might be of my response and my opinion of her.

I first called the 24-year-old woman from my Bible study and asked her what she had most needed when she was in Sarah's shoes.

"Acceptance from my boyfriend's mother," was her reply.

So, following her advice, I called Sarah and made a date to take her to breakfast, where I presented her with a pastel yellow baby layette. I remember cradling it tearfully in my arms, like the child it would someday clothe, when I bought it for Sarah.

"No matter what happens, I want you to have this," I said to her as if she were my own daughter. I also gave her a Bible and read to her the verse in psalms about God knowing her dear baby's unformed body and already ordaining all this child's days.

Sarah's and my relationship was birthed in support, not sermons. I gave her the phone numbers to several Christian counselors, including a faith-based crisis-pregnancy service for single mothers and fathers and urged her and my son to go. Had my son been unwilling to participate, I would have stood in his stead to help emotionally support this mother of my grandchild. (Fortunately, he was an enthusiastic father-in-waiting from day one.)

I also encouraged the two of them to start premarital counseling, which I volunteered to pay for—"no matter what you decide"—to help them tackle issues common to couples. (Many churches offer this service free of charge.)

When Simeon told me that he felt he needed to move in with Sarah to make sure she was protected and supported during this time period, I was shocked when God released me from worry or condemnation over this. *"He's actually doing what Joseph did with Mary,"* I heard Him say to my heart. *"He's protecting her. He's being responsible. He's being the kind of man you taught him to be."*

After hearing that, I called my son and told him that, despite all that had happened, I was proud of him. Despite all those burst bubbles and wrecked carts and now-lame horses, I had hope in the Creator of Plan B.

That plan, I would later find out, included me being invited to witness the birth of my first grandchild, Simeon Braxton Snyder Jr., born December 22, 2004.

10

Your Mother's Shoes

Ouch! Becoming a matriarch
is not necessarily a one-size-
fits-all proposition.

An ounce of mother is worth a pound of clergy.

SPANISH PROVERB

The thief comes only in order to steal and kill and destroy.
I came that they may have and enjoy life, and have it in
abundance (to the full, till it overflows).

JOHN 10:10 AMP

Wal-Mart, with its shopper-filled hustle and bustle, is no place for the faint of heart during the holiday season. But there I was, like the rest of America the week before Christmas, loading up on stocking stuffers.

The crowds and the chaos loomed larger than life, but there was an even louder drumbeat thumping in the background chambers of my heart; something that caused me to stop, abruptly, in the store's Christmas plant department.

In addition to the stocking stuffers I was perfunctorily hefting into my cart, I was also wheeling around a far heavier load—the knowledge that a best friend's mom had died unexpectedly the night before. That's a weight no one wants to carry into Wal-Mart—or anywhere else—during the holiday season or any other time of the year.

My friend's sister had discovered their 70-year-old mother. She'd died peacefully in her sleep. My husband had relayed the message to my cell phone, "Cindy needs you. Her mom just died. She does not sound good."

I, perhaps more than most, understood the ramifications of what this inevitable day represented to Cindy. Like many women our age, she'd been dreading it for a number of years. As her friend of almost 20 years, I had been dreading it with her. And it was about far more than losing a beloved mother.

"My mom is the only person who needs me anymore," Cindy had confided to me less than five years before when my friend's body and mind were feeling the first flickers of perimenopausal introspection. I'd never forgotten her prediction. "There will be no reason for me to live after Mom's gone."

In Cindy's mind, she was dead serious.

Melodramatic as it might sound to anyone not in this situation, Cindy had secretly mused that suicide might be an optional escape from this bewildering part of The Change of Life; the time period when many of us begin to lose our parents and become, for the first time in our lives, orphans. For her, the transition might as well have been called The Change of Life into Death because that was, unfortunately, what this segment of midlife represented to my struggling friend.

For nearly all of us, losing a mother at midlife and stepping into her shoes as the family matriarch is an excruciatingly painful parental paradigm shift—one that can set many of us adrift at a time in life when it seems such an effort just to stay afloat. And it can leave many, if not all, of us sometimes kicking and screaming, "Ouch, one size does *not* fit all" at the tops of our lungs as we desperately try to kick those shoes off.

No longer do we have Mommy to phone when we're in desperate need of emotional thumb sucking. Officially and finally, *we* are now the only mommy we have. No longer do we have Grandma to kiss away life's pains. We are all too often now the only grandmother our families have to turn to. No wonder Cindy felt panicked at the thought of stepping into such cavernous, lonely shoes.

Exacerbating these emotions was the fact that as a devoted, God-fearing, God-loving, stay-at-home mom, Cindy had watched her household dwindle as, one by one, her kids had moved out of the place she'd lovingly tended for more than 20 years. Her now-empty home felt much more like an empty life, metaphorically embodying those empty shoes her mother had just left her to fill.

In corporate terms, Cindy's career had been downsized to the point where she felt she was no longer a needed or valued employee. Simply put, she felt as though she'd lost her job and the job description that went with it. Donning the title of matriarch did *not* feel like a promotion.

Her strong, self-assured, nine-to-five husband loved her dearly, but he couldn't identify with his grief-stricken wife's loss of identity. After all, he still had *his* job, and he couldn't quite grasp how his wife might feel that she'd lost hers. Like many men who find their wives in the throes of The Change, he was bewildered as to how to help.

All this was on my mind as I rolled my cart past hundreds of Wal-Mart poinsettias and Christmas cacti. With holiday carols playing far too cheerily over the store's intercom system, the thought of getting my friend a seasonal flower felt morbidly irreverent. But then I saw them.

Nestled amid the winter foliage, almost hidden from view, was an early shipment of hyacinths; pots and pots of them in varying hues of ivory, pink, and blue. I felt an irrepressible unction to buy her one.

I jerked my cart to a halt.

"Hyacinths? Spring flowers? Isn't that a bit presumptuous? A bit too perky for such a somber event?" I questioned the prompting I've learned to trust over the past quarter of a century with decisions like this.

"Sometimes all you have to give a friend in midlife loss are hyacinths of hope. It's up to Me to make them bloom," hushed the Hot Flash from Heaven like a warm spring breeze in my soul. *"Cindy needs the hope. The future. The promise of spring flowers. The thief comes only in order to steal and kill and destroy. I came that Cindy might have and enjoy life, and have it in abundance until it overflows. Even now. Even in loss. Even in sorrow. And trust Me—the shoes I am forcing her to step into will one day fit like a cozy pair of favorite slippers."* And then it gently added, *"Buy her the plant that hasn't started to bloom."*

Sheesh, I thought to myself as I studied the only pot without opened flowers. It looked so, well, *un*promising with its three spindly sprouts sporting weird-looking, closed-up green buds. Nevertheless, I picked it up and took it to the checkout stand.

Fifteen minutes later I was at my friend's house. Her husband sat across from her at their dining room table as he looked helplessly at me, his eyes imploring me to say something, anything, to lift up his wife's sinking heart. Cindy's eyes were red and puffy from weeping, and the stench of a suicidal-deep depression hung throughout the entire household. It was abundantly clear that the thief was in our midst.

I slid the pot in front of my friend. At first she looked confused. Then a tiny shaft of light sparked in her eyes as she recognized the plant's variety.

"I believe God wanted me to buy you this," I said in half apology at the scrubby chartreuse shoots. I had no idea what to say next.

Cindy stared at it in wonder, and then she said quietly with the slightest flicker of a sad smile at the edges of her mouth, "Mom loved spring flowers. She loved hyacinths. They were her favorite flower of all." At those words, tears began to once again run down her cheeks.

The room was quiet as a crypt as I listened desperately for a Hot Flash to give me the words to fill the silence. Nothing came. I had to wing it and opened my mouth.

"This is where the rubber meets the road with regard to our faith, friend," I whispered as I put my hand on her arm. "We are at the crossroads of age where we are finally forced to accept, trust, and hope that all of this—even death and losing people we love—is as much a part of the preset cycle of life as the blooming of these spring hyacinths."

She looked up at me through her tears as if this was the last thing on earth she wanted to hear.

"Do you see how these buds are unrecognizable?" I continued in totally blind faith that God would save me from saying anything that would further hurt my hurting friend. The words bubbled out.

"That's the way it is after we've planted an elderly mother in the ground and then stepped into her shoes as family matriarch. Life threatens to emerge as something unlovely and unfamiliar for the living left behind. It pushes its way up through the dirty stuff of survival and then blooms into something very different. Different, but beautiful in its own way. As the days ahead unfold, so will these flowers, and day by day you will get more confident that God does, indeed, still have an abundant life for you to live. You will lead your lineage well, dear friend. Just as your mother did before you."

I rested my words, silently praying that God would back them up. The last thing my friend needed was a dead hyacinth.

I wish I could write that everything was immediately better for Cindy. But like growing flowers, this part of The Change takes agonizing, sometimes grief-stricken, time. It would take weeks of wrestling with God and with life and, yes, even with the temptation of suicide, for her to begin to accept that what she had once thought was the end was now a glorious beginning as she tenuously tried on the mantel of matriarch.

But first it would take numerous checkup phone calls from me and others who loved her to keep Cindy on the track toward recovery. It would take repeated daily reminders from her husband and family that they, indeed, still needed her, but in a very different way. They needed her for *who* she was, not for *what* she did for them. True, she was no longer their cook, housekeeper, chauffeur, and laundress, but, continuously they assured her, she was now the revered, much-loved, still-much-needed, grande dame of their gene pool. The maternal anchor of their hearths and hearts. Their matriarch. During it all, the potted plant would sit, almost lifeless, in Cindy's kitchen.

But finally, a couple months later, she called me. In the background were the laughing voices of her grandchildren. "I just had to call you and tell you that the hyacinth is blooming!" she said, her voice vibrant with the knowledge that she was too.

She proceeded to chatter on about what she would need to do with the plant after it was done flowering. At long last, Cindy was thinking ahead to the future—a key hint that the thief had truly been defeated. Over the phone she read to me the instructions on the pot, which told her to put the hyacinth in a cold, dark place for a while, and then bring it out into the light and warmth so that it would repeat the blooming process.

I marveled at the analogy coming out of her own mouth as I saw that this was precisely what God does with each of us in our grief over losing loved ones and then stepping into the unknown. Like the instructions prophesied on the florist's pot, I could see Cindy's heart sprouting with the robust greenery of life. I looked out my window at the still-chilly February snow and then down at my desk calendar to the sunnier months ahead.

I smiled in the comfort that Cindy's hyacinth would, most certainly, bloom again. And the shoes she'd tried so desperately to kick off really were beginning to fit like a pair of perfectly comfy slippers.

● ● ● ● ● ● ●   **MENTAL-PAUSE:**   ● ● ● ● ● ● ●

Attack the Threat of Suicide Aggressively

Don't ever take a friend or loved one's grief-drenched depression lightly, especially if they're talking hopelessly about the value of life. It could be a hint they are mentally flirting with the temptation of suicide and that midlife melancholy has a much-too-firm grip on them.

- Other indicators are:
  - Words like "Nobody needs me. Nobody would miss me if I were gone."
- Actions like:
  - Giving away possessions.
  - Withdrawing from everyday activities such as chatting on the phone and visiting friends.
  - Refusing to make even simple plans for the future—like lunch next week.

If you have reason to believe someone you love is dangerously near the precipice of suicide, become proactive to save them.

Aside from the hyacinths, I made Cindy promise me in writing (with her husband as a witness) and take an oath before God that she would not attempt to harm herself or take her life in any way without first calling him, me, her pastor, or a 24-hour suicide prevention hotline.

I specifically used the words "attempt to harm yourself or take your life in any way" because potential suicides are notoriously crafty at making promises they might later try to get out of. So it's important that your wording eliminates the possibility that they could wiggle around their words.

Verbal or written promises are also an important psychological commitment that many true potential suicides are unwilling to make. So if they refuse to make that commitment, it can also be a hint at their intentions. In addition, for anyone who believes in God, taking an oath before Him is an important spiritual commitment many would be reluctant to make if they were planning to break it. (Had she been unwilling to make these commitments to me, I would have urged Cindy's husband to have her hospitalized immediately.)

At my encouragement, Cindy's husband took her to their doctor and a counselor and got her on medication right away. I also made sure Cindy and her family all had a suicide prevention hotline number that they could call in a crisis. (This toll-free service is available in most large cities—check for it in yours. You'll likely find it in the business section of your phone book under "suicide." Or call your nearest mental health care agency. They should be able to point you towards 24-hour resources in your city.)

For a number of weeks Cindy was never left alone, and Cindy's husband wisely insisted that she always carry a cell phone so that he and I and many other people who loved her could frequently check in on her. Then we all wove a web of heavy-duty, down-in-the-trenches prayer for Cindy that continued until thoughts of suicide lost their power in her life.

Several years later, she has lost 30 lbs, looks 10 years younger, and has a vibrant enjoyment of life that centers around giving to her husband, her grown kids, her many grandkids, and her even more abundant friends.

She now believes that they all still very much need her—but in ways quite different from when she was a younger woman, before she became the magnificent matriarch that she is today.

Puttin' the Pursuit Back in Papa

Yes, old dogs (and even older husbands) can learn new romance-enhancing tricks.

It would have made a great cartoon if someone would have drawn it. Except the subject matter was way too serious, way too personal, and not one bit comedic.

But cut me some slack here.

I had to chuckle a bit when I pictured the two confused farmer-type men talking in that aw-shucks manner that farmer-type guys sometimes talk in, their hands shoved deep in their Carhartt coverall pockets, the toes of their heavy work boots doodling lines in the mud as they looked at the ground rather than make too much eye contact. Especially when one of those farmer-type guys was my husband.

Only the two old dogs—my hubby and my neighbor—weren't scratching their heads over the price of last year's wheat or discussing the sticker shock on modern farm machinery that day. They were talking a new kind of middle-aged guy-speak; one that's been coming up a lot lately in my husband's musings with fellow males. The subject matter? "Women who wander." It's become a term I've coined for those seemingly dependably wedded women who up and leave their husbands after sometimes decades of marriage.

In this case, they were discussing why a fellow farmer type was, after 30 or so years of marriage, now sleeping single in a double bed. His wife had wandered—big-time—and run off with a man she'd met on the Internet.

"I just don't get it," my husband said to me in bed later that night when he described the conversation he'd had with the farmer friend who knew the couple far better than we. Said friend had assured my husband that he couldn't think of any possible reason that the woman might have had to leave.

"Why, he spoiled her rotten, built her a house, took her on trips..." my man's voice trailed off repeating what his friend had said as if that defined the perfect husband. His unspoken deduction? The woman had simply hit menopause, flipped out, and left. I shook my head as I winced at male naïveté.

But not before I thought long and hard about the laws of nature.

Because we live in the country, I'm privileged to see those laws play out in wildlife's annual rituals, and I've learned a lot by observing them.

From my kitchen window I've watched buck deer chase down does in a giddy, nose-to-the-ground, throw-caution-to-the-wind type of pursuit so intoxicating that it leaves them oblivious to the dangers of the hunters hunting them.

I've marveled over monogamous male geese as they defend our pond's nesting place—and their feathered female life mates—at all cost, chasing down intruders far larger than themselves and never losing sight of the object of their affection, which they continue to pine after and protect, season after season, year after year.

I see wild turkeys puff their plumage and strut their stuff for hens who'd never give them the time of day if the old coots were vegging on their Lazy Boys in dirty boxer shorts with clickers in their hands, er, claws. But, oops, I'm getting ahead of myself here.

Wild male animals seem to instinctually know something that older human ones often choose to ignore or forget: If you don't stay in hot pursuit, you lose the prize.

So it was with this in mind that I repeated to my husband the Hot Flash from Heaven that was now roaring through my feminine heart like a flock of squawking geese, *"It's not about possessions or presents. It's about pursuit. Pursuit wins a woman's heart. And it's pursuit that continues to keep it."*

And I thought back to our own marriage of more than a quarter of a century.

There's nothing like the "double-decade hump"—the time period when emptying ovaries, wombs, estrogen, nests, and marriages converge—to remind an old girl of what she's often long been missing. Pursuit. Hot pursuit, if you will. The pulse-quickening look in her husband's eyes that lets her know she's the most important thing to him in his universe next to God.

Single guys get it. And we can blame it on hormones and/or horniness, but somehow they know if they don't passionately pursue their princess, she'll wind up as someone else's prom queen.

So why is it that once the rings are exchanged men forget all that?

I call it "head-mount syndrome," and a couple years ago I explained it like this to my newly married son-in-law who loves to hunt: "The man sets his sights on his dream woman and, believe me, when he does, she knows it. She knows it by his tone of voice; the tenderness and flirtatiousness in it when he addresses her. The look in his eyes; the softness and kindness in them as they search out hers." I furthered, "She senses his body language; relaxed and warm, not stiff or impatient, when he affectionately interacts with her. And she's acutely aware of both his physical and emotional movement *toward*—not *away*—from their relationship. As a result she's acutely aware whether it is cocooned gently in a crevasse of caresses or petrified into stony complacency."

I continued to explain to my son-in-law how the stealthy hunter does whatever it takes to capture the prize of his life. He persistently pursues, courts, and woos her until he's chased down her heart. Finally, his consistency and perseverance pay off.

She falls in love and makes the choice to risk giving away her heart, her body, and, in many ways, her life. At the wedding ceremony he slips a ring on her finger and prides himself on getting the very big and important job done. Then sometime shortly thereafter, he tightens up his ammo-belt and looks around for other equally impressive big game to pursue—progeny, promotions, possessions, and pastimes—leaving an often bewildered and lonely wife in his wake.

My son-in-law gave me his own deer-in-the-headlights look, but I pressed on, not wanting him to make the same mistakes I'd seen so many other men—including my own hunter-hubby—do.

I explained to him the revelation I recently got about that age-old myth that says women marry a man thinking they'll change him. Frankly, I think that's—for lack of better words—a crock, and here's why.

All the women I know (and, believe me, I've met *hundreds* of them over my five decades on this planet) married their men thinking just the opposite: That here was such an extraordinary guy, so deeply ga-ga over them, that he'd stay just the same, sweet, pursuing pursuer the lady had fallen in love with in the first place.

These women truly trusted. In many ways they gambled their entire lives upon the firm belief that the man *wouldn't* change. That he wouldn't stop making those tender middle-of-the-day phone calls to say, "Honey, I just wanted you to know that I'm thinking of you." That he wouldn't quit leaving those little notes, bringing those bouquets of wildflowers, greeting his girl with kisses, smiles, and kind, unrushed words after a day away from her. In short, that the guy wouldn't quit pursuing the gal.

But rather quickly (many have confided to me that it happened almost as soon as the honeymoon was over) the, well, honeymoon was over. The baffled brides were then left to sadly watch as their beloveds resighted their passions in on other things to conquer. And before too long, the women would be metaphorically relegated to the position of very dusty head-mounts on their husbands' equally metaphoric trophy room wall.

Soon, though, each woman would go through a similar metamorphosis as her broken heart would become distracted by day planners, diapers, and dustpans. And each left-behind lady would discover herself rather adept at relegating her yearnings for closeness, intimacy, and pursuit to the category of "unmet dreams." *This must be the status quo of adulthood,* she finally says bravely to herself as she trods dutifully on as a busy mom or childless career woman.

Then, one day many years later, the kids move out or job pressures ease, calendars, homes, and lives quiet down, and the midlife woman wakes up and sees her emotional anorexia for what it really is—poverty of passion.

She may make one last plea to her husband that they do more things together, that they share more romance, maybe see a counselor or attend a marriage seminar, but more often than not, her voice has grown hoarse over the years of begging him for these things. Many of the women I've known, and this includes some very strong Christian ones, have simply dissolved off into the darkness of divorce with their disconnected husbands clueless until the women announce to them that they're leaving.

One of the male exceptions to this rule, a very dialed-in clinical psychologist friend of mine who counsels many of these types of women, gets the credit for confirming to me that there are often weighty reasons for this.

I'll never forget the day he leaned forward in his office chair, looked directly in my eyes, and said the seven words that finally validated the yearnings I had nearly deleted from my databank of desires. Though they were his words, I instantly recognized them as much more. They were a Hot Flash from Heaven that applied not only to me, but to all women.

"You were made to be pursued, Ronna," he announced and those Hot Flash-laden words thundered into my heart with as much power as if he were Moses decreeing one of the Ten Commandments.

You see, I, too, had been a very dusty head-mount on a very flat and lonely wall for far, far too long. I'd become so dusty, in fact, that my vision had been shrouded behind my own glass-eyed stares as I'd blindly watched the marital pursuit I'd always longed for stay strangely out of reach.

Like many of my counselor friend's clientele, I had been "gut-shot and left for dead" (that's hunting vernacular for "abandoned," girl-friend) the day after our wedding. We were brand-new Christians, stupidly young, and this was the second marriage for both of us. Because of that, we had opted for a quickie jeans-and-T-shirt-style marriage and an overnight honeymoon at a local motel.

My romance-challenged farmer-type husband had explained to me that he needed to get back to feed the chickens in the morning. I am totally serious! And I was so in love that I didn't recognize the announcement for the huge red flag it was. A signal that something had just abruptly upped me on my husband's priority list. In my striv-ing to start out my marriage as a scripturally inspired submissive wife, I acquiesced without voicing my hurt. That was my first mistake. My continued voicelessness would set a painful pattern to our relationship that allowed our marriage to, in many ways, stew on the back burner of pursuit for two decades.

Oh, sure. Like many women, I'd *tried* to speak. But when I'd tried to explain to my husband my need for passionate pursuit, I'd been easily silenced by accusations of insecurity and discontentment. After all, no woman wants to be thought of as insecure or discontented by her husband. It makes her sound and feel so, so, so, unpursuit worthy. Church teachings that sometimes fuzzed the line between being a rebellious wife, on the one hand, and assertively requesting growth in my marriage, on the other, further stifled my voice and confused my thinking.

So you can imagine how freeing those seven little words were when spoken to me by a handsome, happily married, middle-aged male Christian counselor who was a church leader in his own right.

In order to illustrate his statement, he offered up the human anatomy, pointing to the way our bodies were constructed by a very shrewd Creator.

"The woman's heart is kind of like her body: It's built to *receive* the man's," he explained as tactfully as he could to me that day in his office. "And the man's is made to go *into* the woman. To *implant* life into her. And that's all kinds of life, not just the physical act of creating a baby. It's joy. Laughter. Love. Fun. Friendship. The man's body, just like his heart, can't implant life in the woman—physically, emotionally, or spiritually—without pursuit. And just as the woman is made to be pursued by the man, the man is made to pursue her."

Needless to say, it wouldn't be long before I would drag my husband in to hear those life-affirming, marriage-enhancing, woman-wooing words. And I thank God that he was man enough to hear and receive them. And that he would then begin to act upon them by deliberately resetting his sights on the marriage. That simple act gradually started a major shift toward treating me like a prize he didn't want to lose. And I could definitely feel it.

After so many years of trying to explain to him my needs, I was amazed at how quickly he instinctually grasped—without much detailed explanation—what the word "pursuit" looks like to a woman. Almost overnight the ol' dog learned new tricks, reverting back to his long-buried "hunting" instincts of so long ago. He increased his eye contact, affection, attention, and openness. He ditched the distance he'd often hidden behind and made a conscious decision to ramp up his desire to be vulnerable and transparent.

While words like "intimacy" and "connection" are often too ethereal, nebulous, and formidable for the male mind to grasp, "pursuit" is a word most men get almost instantly. It must go back to the hunter-gatherer in all of them. Speak the word "pursuit" to most men and many, like my husband, will finally sigh with relief. "Ahhh-haaaaa, so *that's* what the ol' gal needs." The wise ones will think it over and come to the conclusion, "Now that's one thing I *can* do." Something inside them tells them, maybe even compels them, that they, like their female counterparts, were made for it.

The Old Testament's Jacob got this whole pursuit business. And he didn't forget it over the seven years he indentured himself (that's Old Testament talk for "worked his tail off"), to Laban to win the gruff ol' geezer's youngest daughter, Rachel. Nor did Jacob forget it when the deceptive Laban fed Jacob a substitute bride as Laban sneaked his older, heavily veiled daughter, Leah—rather than Rachel—into the wedding tent that first night of their honeymoon. I find it interesting that the Bible describes pursuit so aptly in Jacob's story on the pages of Genesis: "Jacob served seven years to *get* Rachel, but they seemed like only a few days to him because of his love for her" (Genesis 29:20).

When Jacob awoke to Leah's uncomely face instead of Rachel's and then confronted his sneaky new father-in-law, Jacob agreed to work another seven years to earn the hand of his beloved.

You see, pursuit doesn't keep track of effort. Or time. Or cost. Or paybacks. Pursuit runs on the limitless pulse of passion.

Another one of my husband's friends demonstrated this more aptly than any self-help book could. Gary had been a busy CEO of a hugely successful company all his 30-plus years of marriage, jet-setting all over the globe to meet important clientele. He'd been so busy, in fact, that he was more comfortable in a boardroom than the bedroom of his own home. Over the years I'd watched Gary's unpursued wife erode into a life-sized but lifeless facsimile of what she'd once been. Her body had put on copious amounts of weight erroneously trying to feed her heart as it slowly shriveled with emotional starvation.

"You mark my words," I'd told my husband ten years earlier, "Their marriage won't make it."

My husband guffawed at the notion, pointing to their decades together as if to prove me wrong. Two years after the couple's last child left the nest, Gary was reeling with the news that his wife was leaving him. He begged to meet with her counselor, but it was too late. She'd been seeing the counselor alone for years because Gary had always insisted that his wife's deep sadness was *her* problem, not his, and he'd refused to go.

"You can win her back, Gary," I told him one night in a rare heart-to-heart conversation as his own was breaking. "Almost any woman can be rewon by pursuit if it's not only consistent but persistent."

And so Gary tried. For about three days. But then he became angry that his wife wasn't instantly responding. And then he began blaming her. Not himself, mind you. Just her. After less than a week he abruptly quit pursuing.

"That's hardly pursuit," I said to my husband as he watched dumbfounded at how little effort his wounded friend was willing to expend on behalf of a triple-decade relationship that was worth far more. We both were tempted to believe Gary simply didn't know how to pursue.

But then an interesting thing happened. Shortly after the divorce was final, guy meets gal. More aptly put, Gary met a woman he decided he wanted very much. And then, gee, all of a sudden the guy miraculously *remembered* how to pursue. And he did it quite well, I might add. Flowers, dinners, notes in her purse, sweet nothings in her ear, unhurried time together, the whole shebang. And, yup, he caught her. But this time, unbeknownst to Gary, he got his hands full. You see, he hooked a middle-aged woman whose own Change of Life and Hot Flashes from Heaven have taught her the imperative importance of the word "pursuit" in a relationship. And she's not willing to settle for anything less for the rest of her life.

One can only hope Gary gets it because I know for sure that old dogs, like old husbands, can learn new tricks and chuck bad relational habits. But in Gary's case, only time will tell.

Whatever the case, I know for a fact that he's in for a big surprise. His new meno-mama will never, ever settle for hanging rights on someone's trophy room wall.

So I guess I was very fortunate that my counselor friend taught me *and* my dear husband the "P" word in a way that we both could grasp at the same time. I was also fortunate that it was a wise Christian counselor, and not some trophyless hunter on yet another safari, who originally spoke that "pursuit" word to me because, frankly, unpursued women are very vulnerable women. Thus, our farmer friend's empty bed.

But rather than look to other men, I'd chosen an equally harmful alternative. Like Gary's wife, I'd turned my desperate needs inward, berating myself for my husband's lack of pursuit. This behavior manifested itself in a self-deprecating depression that I somehow managed to keep hidden from most of the world. "If I were just sexier, sweeter, smarter, stronger, more submissive," I had long-reasoned with myself, "my husband would want to pursue me."

While Gary's wife eventually learned differently, I'd missed the point entirely. And my counselor friend was quick to point this out.

When God created Adam, he explained to me one day, He took a look at His handiwork and saw what was missing in the big guy's life. God said, "It's not good for the man to be alone" (Genesis 2:18). Then He created the perfect solution. He made estrogen-filled Eve. One woman, not ten, I must note. A real woman, not an airbrushed, Photoshop'd fantasy, I'll also add. And it's critical to recognize that God didn't make Eddie, the hunting buddy, to be Adam's companion. Nor Alex, the football fanatic friend. (Nor did he give Adam and Alex season tickets so they could spend the rest of their life together on the 50 yard line). And it's even more important to note that God didn't see Adam's need and send him dirty boxers, a television set, and five clickers. Why, He didn't even make a career or a big fat IRA to complete Adam.

He made—are you ready for this earth-shattering news, ladies?—a woman. A woman not unlike you and me, girlfriend. A flawed female dumb enough to fall for a single forbidden piece of fruit on a tree, yes. But a woman that He nonetheless described in the very first chapter of Genesis as made "in the image of God" (Genesis 1:27). A gender He thought so highly of that He declared men should leave everything and cleave to their wives in one-flesh unity that leaves nothing else but God Himself in first place. No room for cleaving to anything else, from cash to careers to clickers, says the Scripture. Cleave to your wife, says God. Webster's defines the word "cleave" even further with synonyms like "cling, hang on to, stick to, embrace, remain attached." Sounds more than a little like pursuit, doesn't it?

What affirming words. Words that finally spoke to my X chromosome-charged heart that perhaps the woman's deep desire to feel pursued just might be a sacred aspect of her personality born in her own God-Father's heart. Let's call it "The DNA of Divine Desire"; something maybe *He* implanted into us, the daughters of Eve, for the sole purpose of bringing out the very best in our Adams. For enhancing their softer side. For growing and nurturing the kindness and tenderness that God designed them to feel.

It was here, at this precious crossroads called The Change of Life, that I realized that my gender need not be embarrassed or apologetic for those yearnings for pursuit. They do not make us weaklings. They do not brand us insecure, discontented shrews.

They make us women.

And that, and that alone, makes us worthy of even more than a lifetime of pulse-pounding pursuit. I think Adam would agree. I *know* Eve would.

● ● ● ● ● ● ● **MENTAL-PAUSE:** ● ● ● ● ● ● ●

Examine Thyself, Then Pursue Pursuit

Got an ol' dog who's hung your head on the trophy room wall for far too long? Maybe it's time to teach him some new tricks.

The first thing to do is dust your own self-image off and take a close look at who you really are: A woman made in the image of God, without whom your husband is not nearly the man he could—or should—be. A woman Christ pursued so ardently that He endured a cross for you some 2000 years before your conception.

If you've exhausted your vocabulary with your husband using words like "connection," "intimacy," "affection," and that even scarier term for guys—"romance"—try the word "pursuit" when expressing your needs to him. Feel free to quote my counselor friend's theory about male and female anatomy.

For some reason that's a visual that brings great clarity to the word "pursuit" for many males. And feel equally free to ask your husband to read this chapter.

Then ascribe to the KISS (Keep It Simple, Sister) method of getting your relationship on track.

In my household, I try hard not to lecture or make complicated edicts. After all, if I was made for pursuit, my husband was just as equally made to pursue. In so many ways it's already in him to know what to do. It's just that doing life gets so distracting.

Therefore the five little words, "Honey, I'm not feeling pursued," are usually all that's needed to tell my husband that, for whatever reasons, I feel like I'm back on the back burner of his priorities.

But at the same time don't expect the ol' guy to be a mind reader. In very simple language and sentences, I had to explain to Bill what pursuit looks like to me.

"When you gently touch me while we're passing in the hall," I explained to him one day, "your affection lets me know I'm valued and desired—that I'm pursued." He puffed up proudly like a peacock in full plumage when he started doing things like this.

It was so adorable to watch, and I tried to reward him with lots of positive verbal affirmations like, "Honey, I noticed it when you touched me in the hall today. You made me feel like such a queen when you did that." (More puffing and plumage.)

He has come to find out that, unlike his initial conversation with his farmer friend, I'm not asking for expensive things like a new house or a fancy vacation.

I, like all the rest of the women I know, hunger only for the most valuable thing our husbands possess. Something that's absolutely free for the giving: Their hearts in pursuit of ours as they willingly put down the TV clickers—or anything else they're holding tightly onto—and tenderly cradle our hands in their own.

12

Perfuming the Past

Leaving behind fragrant legacies while we've still got time.

● ● ● ● ● ● ● **POWER SURGES** ● ● ● ● ● ● ●

An apology is the superglue of life.
It can repair just about anything.

LYNN JOHNSTON

I have everything I need and am amply supplied,
now that I have received from Epaphroditus the gifts you sent
me. [They are] the fragrant odor of an offering and sacrifice
which God welcomes and in which He delights.

PHILIPPIANS 4:18 AMP

I smelled the intoxicating perfume as soon as I entered the store. I hadn't smelled it in years. And it had no place in a cheesy little neighborhood grocery store's produce department, so it was not as though I was expecting it to hit me so powerfully. But I knew what it was even before I found its source, lurking between overripe tomatoes and a few little Boston ferns.

It's the smell of gardenias, I smiled to myself. *It's the smell of my father.*

Then the Hot Flash hit.

"Your life leaves behind a fragrance long after you're gone. Make sure it's a sweet one."

We all have fragrances left over from childhood—those special smells that, when inhaled, instantly propel us back into the past. To this day I can sniff a certain kind of rubbery plastic and my mind translates the message I get in my nose into the unmistakable memory in my head of a new doll at Christmastime. Even though I am now more than halfway through my life, within seconds I am once again a little girl opening Christmas presents with my family back in the '50s.

But it's not really the new dolls I remember with such fondness. And it's not the other presents, either. It's the love of my family as we joyfully shared the holidays that floods my memory bank.

And then there's a certain odor I can sometimes discern in funky old neighborhood markets. It's a yeasty kind of smell that can't be found in the slick new superstores of today. As soon as it hits the memory receptors in my head, I picture my paternal grandmother who, when I was lucky enough to visit her clear across the state from my home in Seattle, would always walk me down to the nearby grocery to purchase the bakery's first offerings of the day. The potpourri of pastries would hit our noses as soon as we entered the store.

But it's not the baked goods I remember, either. It's the warmth I had in my heart when I was around the woman who made me—her firstborn grandchild—feel as though I walked on water.

In the same vein, my dad, her only son, began giving me gardenias when I was too young to know or appreciate how delicate and expensive the waxy white flowers are.

I remember the first single snowy bloom he presented to me in a fancy gold floral box. I think it was my twelfth birthday. My mother showed me how to float it in a crystal bowl of water, and we put the elegant centerpiece on the coffee table for the entire family to enjoy. Every so often I'd plunge my nose into the glass and take a huge whiff of the gardenia's fragrance. I couldn't imagine how one simple flower could carry such a potent perfume, one that would forever after remind me of Dad's gifts to me.

I guess it shouldn't have been any surprise when, a few years later, as an awkward 16-year-old, I would save my hard-earned babysitting money to buy the extravagantly expensive fragrance that usually only older, wealthier, more sophisticated women could afford in those days. It was called White Shoulders. Its key ingredient? Gardenias.

Somewhere along the way of my father giving me those costly flowers, I'd clearly gotten his message to me: "You are worth it, Daughter, because I love you."

Over a decade later, Dad would build on that message even further.

While he was great at making me feel loved, my father made a critical mistake during my early teen years that ultimately interfered significantly with every other aspect of his life and personality. Shortly after he gave me that first gardenia, Dad toppled deep into the abyss of alcoholism.

By the time I realized he had a problem, I was starting my high school years. I remember the feelings of powerlessness as I watched my family life literally crumble around my two siblings and me. Mom would eventually divorce Dad. He would marry another woman, one who knew nothing of his addiction. And none of us would smell the fragrance of gardenias for some time to come.

A couple years after his remarriage, I received a phone call from my dad's second wife. Now savvy to his alcoholism, she begged me to help her help my father. This was the early '70s and the word "intervention" had yet to be coined.

Looking back, she'd laid a lot on my 22-year-old shoulders. But for some unexplained reason, I knew exactly what to do. We orchestrated our own version of an intervention, of forcing things to a head to get the addict to face reality.

I made some phone calls to drug and alcohol treatment facilities across the state and found out that, without a court order, there was no way that I, or anyone else, could force my dad to enter one. In order to do that, we'd have to go through a lengthy uphill legal process and prove that my dad was a danger to himself and to society, something I wasn't sure we could prove or pay for.

So I did the next best thing. I called my father's boss. Fortunately, the man had a lot of compassion and an open mind. He agreed to hold my father's job for him for as long as necessary while he went into treatment. He also agreed to wield the ultimate hammer. He would stand behind me when I told my father that if he didn't get the help he needed, he would lose his job forever.

We assembled the troops—other relatives who loved my dad and had the nerve it took to join in the intervention. In addition to Dad's boss, a staff counselor from the rehabilitation facility joined us to keep the encounter as calm and loving as possible. It was he who would usher my emotionally ambushed father off in the hospital's car with the suitcase already packed by my stepmother tucked discreetly in the backseat.

This was no storybook intervention with Dad cheerfully seeing the error of his ways and jumping excitedly into the counselor's waiting vehicle. I later learned from the counselors that these kinds of events seldom are. And it's that woeful reason that often prevents loved ones from doing just what we had done.

But years later, the most important things remained. Dad *did* get into that car; albeit so angry it would take him several months to speak to any of us again. Dad *did* finally face the truth that he was an alcoholic. Dad *did* sober up and reach out in repentance to God and to his family and friends. And, most important, Dad stayed that way until he died.

It was for those very reasons that I stopped everything I was doing in that grocery store that day to pick up the lone gardenia plant. I buried my face in the petals, and as my nose drank in the aromatic bouquet, I remembered Dad and all the times he'd lovingly given me plants just like this one.

And you know what? Not a single one of those good memories is marred by the aching pain that alcoholism can etch on a family's life. And with good reason. Because in his sobriety, Dad gave me an even greater gift than gardenias. You see, he paid a price for me and others he loved. He sacrificed his desire for alcohol for our desire for his sobriety. He chose to do the right thing instead of the easy thing. He overcame his weakness, and in doing so, he freed me to remember him with pride once again—not pity or pain.

Perhaps because of that, it was even easier for me, just three years later, to believe that another man had done the same thing for me. His name? Jesus Christ. He, too, paid a price on a cross that said to me, "You are worth it, Daughter, because I love you."

If midlife teaches us anything, it is that true repentance means not only saying sorry, but staying sorry, and demonstrating by your actions that you truly are. Dad taught me that, not by the flowers he sent, but by the sweet-smelling gift of a changed life. In doing so, he expanded even further on the message he'd given me as a young girl with a lesson that would carry me into middle age and beyond.

Thankfully, Dad hadn't responded with the lame excuse many older people come up with regarding their past mistakes in life: "It's too late." It wasn't too late, I'd soon learn. It was just in time. He passed away, totally unexpectedly, only a few years later at the very young age of 54. And I was comforted that he had "done business with God" before it was too late.

And now at virtually the same age, I, too, look at things I've done in my life that I wish I could change, that I wish I could do over. And I think of Dad and the lesson he left me about the fragrances we leave behind after we're gone. I think about the power of midlife repentance. Of doing things differently and, in many ways, erasing the stinging pain of the past. For ourselves and for those we love.

I took one last sniff of that gardenia plant and then set it in my basket. I couldn't find a price tag on it anywhere. I didn't care. I'd already decided that I was buying it, no matter what the cost. The fragrance was truly priceless to me. Both my earthly father and my heavenly One had reassured me years ago: *You are worth it, Daughter, because I love you.*

As I gently lifted the gardenia onto the checkout stand, I said a silent prayer; one, I'm sure, not commonly prayed in grocery store checkout lanes. "Lord, may I, too, leave behind that very same fragrance for my own loved ones to inhale forever."

● ● ● ● ● ● ● ● **MENTAL-PAUSE:** ● ● ● ● ● ● ● ●

What Does Your Past Smell Like to Others?

Do you have things you need your loved ones to forgive you of? Do you have mistakes you've committed that may forever affect their fragrant memories of you?

Do business first with God and then with your loved ones. Do the work that it takes to get rid of, and stay rid of, the stuff you're sorry for. Then make sure you do it for the rest of your life. Tell them you're sorry. A powerful apology is one that owns the mistake verbally.

For example, when I realized that my already serious, first born son had grown into a much too serious adult, I felt terrible for the part I'd played in making him even more so. Painful and embarrassing as it was, I told him, "Son, I should have taught you to have more fun. You didn't need to be taught to be more responsible and hardworking. You were born that way. I feel as though I missed the boat in not teaching you to be more laid-back and playful. I couldn't teach what I didn't know. I am so very sorry. Please forgive me." Then I tried to demonstrate my repentance by changing my behavior.

As a result of my conversation with my son, I now do everything in my power to be lighthearted and joyful when I'm around him as a reminder that if I can change, he can too.

Dad taught me something else about leaving fragrant legacies. He taught me it's never too late or too early to do the right thing. When I felt the unction to write my dad one of those kinds of letters you'd want to write to a loved one if you knew it was the last thing you were going to say to that person, I did so. Five days after mailing it, my father died in completely good health while taking a nap. The last words he uttered to a friend before he took that final siesta were, "I've been praying to God, and I've never felt so much peace in all my life."

And no wonder. The day I arrived home from his funeral I checked the mailbox and found a loving letter he'd written in response to my own. It was postmarked with the day of his death, and he had mailed it just hours before he passed away.

Now *that* is a gift more fragrant than any gardenia, and one I'll breathe in for the rest of my life.

13

Midlife "Marymaking"

Quick, Doc, are there meds for middle-aged, type A Martha-ism?

● ● ● ● ● ● ● ● **POWER SURGES** ● ● ● ● ● ● ●

The time to relax is when you don't have time for it.

ATTRIBUTED TO BOTH JIM GOODWIN AND SYDNEY J. HARRIS

"Martha, Martha," the Lord answered, "you are worried and upset about many things, but only one thing is needed. Mary has chosen what is better, and it will not be taken away from her."

LUKE 10:41-42

E-mail aside, as a middle-aged freelance writer who lives in a beautiful, but very rural location, days can go by before I talk with a single human being outside of my own family.

With little input from the outside world, besides the occasional letter to the editor written by some reader and forwarded to me by the publications I've written for, I often find myself questioning whether I'm really fulfilling my true purpose in life. Like my many years of staying at home to raise and homeschool our four kids, my walk of faith has been so solitary that it sometimes seems worthless and unrecognized by the world's standards.

God hasn't been helping me in these midlife matters much, either.

"Don't you get it, girl? It's about who you ARE, Ronna, not about what you DO. It's about how YOU need ME, not about how I need YOU." I'd been hearing this tender but insistent Hot Flash from Heaven reverberate for what seemed like months now in my hormonally hampered psyche. And, frankly, it had been bugging me. That was until recently, when everything just sort of seemed to make sense.

I'd been sitting in my living room chair as I've done most mornings since I became a Christian more than a quarter of a century ago. It's my in lieu of caffeine morning wakeup ritual. Blurry-eyed, I make myself a fake cappuccino (that's the kind with no sugar, no caffeine, no fat, and, well, no fun) and park myself in my cozy leather chair with my Bible. Sometimes I read. Lots of times I repent. (I happen to have a lot of that to do.) Mostly I pray. And always I try real, real hard to listen. To listen for that Hot Flash that creeps into my heart with the darnedest of thoughts.

"So, Ronna, if all I asked of you today was to sit at My feet and do nothing, like Mary instead of Martha, would you do it? COULD you do it?"

I wanted so badly to say yes as I thought about the biblical story of the two sisters with very different personalities. Martha was the New Testament's equivalent to Martha Stewart on steroids, and she was one of the main players in the Bible's rendition of *Guess Who's Coming to Dinner.* Only her important dinner guest was Jesus, and she was running around, very Marthalike, striving to pull off the big event. That was so me.

Her totally right-brained sister, Mary, was completely oblivious to her own social faux pas. All Mary wanted to do was sit at Jesus' feet and—get this—listen to Him! Can you imagine her audacity? That was so *not* me at the time. And Mary's "merry" behavior made Martha even crazier as she shifted into hormonal overdrive.

"For heaven's sake, Jesus," whined Martha, "tell Mary to get off her behind and help me." I'm paraphrasing here, but basically Martha had a majorly full day planner, and she had jobs she needed to get done for God.

Boy, do I identify with Martha. Mary was entirely too laid-back about this serving God and fulfilling my purpose stuff for me to see much of myself in her.

Nevertheless, there was no one else in the living room that morning. Those questions from the heavens had obviously been meant only for me. I couldn't ignore them.

Sure, I could do that, Lord, I wanted to reply in my typical bold, recovering type A voice, desperately convincing myself I really meant it. But could I? Could I just simply sit still and believe that even if I did nothing, maybe *especially* if I did nothing, that God could use an old broad like me? I decided that, at least for just *one* day, it might not kill me.

Midlife does that to women, you know. The Change empowers us to do things we neither had the time, nor the temperament, for in youth when our main goal was to conquer our own little corner of the world.

So there I sat. In my living room chair. Still. Quiet. Breathing. Listening. For a long, long time. I never left that chair, except to refuel my cup with that shabby substitute for real coffee. Then the phone rang. *Might as well answer it,* I thought to myself. I didn't have anything else to do, right?

It was Melissa, a woman I'd met the year before. In our very first meeting she'd poured out her heart to me and told me much about her life. Her marriage of 20 years had digressed into a loveless one, maintained largely for the sake of their kids. I had shared with her that God *is* love, and without Him the emotion's pretty elusive. I'd let her know how, even as Christians, my husband and I had had our own troubled times and that counseling with the right counselor can be a true godsend. But most of all, I encouraged her to give God a try in her own personal life and in her marriage, and then I gave her a Bible. Every few months throughout the past year, we'd touched base with one another, but our conversations had never gone deeper than the first one.

Melissa had liked my weekly newspaper column called "Hot Flashes" in the local paper and decided to call and tell me so. We discussed the topic of the most recent one, about the amount of effort and commitment it takes to continue to stay in a long-term loving marriage. "You don't even have to always feel like you love someone," I told her. "You just have to *want to* love them."

I could hear in her voice the shock of thinking about "wanting to" love her husband again after so many years of coldness. And I marveled at the insights The Big M gives to midlife perspectives.

"Matter of fact, Melissa, you don't even have to *want* to," I added pushing the envelope even further. "You just have to *want to* 'want to.'" We both chuckled over the play on words, but Melissa was beginning to grasp the idea that love is a heart matter, ruled by the brain, but set on course, sometimes solely, by the mouth.

The Change had brought me to the point that I now knew that saying "I *want* to love you" often has the power to open a door in the heart, even after years of frigid closure.

By the time our lengthy conversation ended, Melissa had caught the vision and was thinking she just might give it a try. I suggested she have her husband read my column and then tell him that she was making the choice to "want to" love him again. "Maybe I could just want to want to?" she asked with the tiniest little voice full of tentative hope.

I laughed back and assured her that that was probably good enough with God and He'd likely meet her heart right where it was at. I whistled out a long breath as I hung up the phone.

"Wow, God, that was cool," I said into the stillness. I felt that maybe I'd actually made a difference in someone else's life. And that difference had come as a direct result of being still enough to be useful. Then I snuggled even deeper into my chair to do nothing again.

The phone rang minutes later. In Bible studies with homeless women, I've had a little experience counseling them about the issues many of them face, including abusive spouses. My nonhomeless friends know that, and every once in a while the lessons I've gleaned from my work with the homeless come in handy in the "normal" world. This was such a time.

Jill was calling on behalf of her friend Sally, a brand-new Christian whose husband had not only threatened to kill her but described in vivid detail how he was going to do it. While I'd never met Sally, Jill asked if I'd talk with the sobbing woman she had on a three-way phone connection with me. As I agreed, Jill introduced us over the phone and then tactfully hung up as the timid-voiced woman and I chatted.

Before I said anything further, I made sure that Sally had the city's domestic violence (DV) shelter's 24-hour hotline number run by the YWCA. I explained that she could call them 24/7, and they would even pick her and her children up and put them in safe hiding. I also gave her the phone number of the Y's free counseling service for DV victims and encouraged her to make an appointment right away.

Over the next couple of hours I verbally held her hand. It was full of jumbled emotions. Like many victims of abuse, she was very confused about what was the truth and what was craftily camouflaged falsehood spewed out by her abuser and still stewing in her self-image. She was doubly entrenched in the confusion because she'd been with the man so long.

For years she had held herself together for the sake of her children who were, at long last, finally leaving the nest. No coincidence here. That's the precise time when many abused women finally find the courage to rethink the way their marriage has been for so many years and then decide they want that midlife word we love so much: Change.

She had no idea what rights she had as a woman, a wife, a human being, and, most important, a child of God. Adding to this cacophony of confusion was the deepest deception of all, one forged upon her by well-meaning but out to lunch Christians. That God somehow might not love her as much if she left her husband of nearly 20 years. These were Christians who cluelessly brushed off her allegations of abuse and didn't dive deep enough in her confessional to find out that the man was actually relishing in planning his wife's death—a no-brainer that true abuse is actually happening. And that something even worse might soon occur.

As surely as I'd encouraged Melissa to risk her heart by moving emotionally closer to her husband of 20 years, I urged Sally to draw back and seek safety. As emphatically as I'd assured Melissa that God could warm a heart frozen by the iciness of bitterness, I comforted Sally that perhaps God would quench the flames of her husband's hot hatred by leading her away from the source of the fire—him.

When I finally hung up the phone, I was emotionally, spiritually, and physically drained. I had given all I had to give in those two phone calls, and I had yet to move out of that living room chair. The day was nearly gone, but it felt well spent.

I marveled at the two very different messages—almost exact opposite ones—delivered that day to two very different middle-aged women I barely knew. If I'd been a Martha that day, tearing through my to-do list as I'd originally planned, I doubt I would have been in the right state of mind or spirit to hear, or to pass on, what I felt might be helpful guidance for the two women. It took a spiritual sharpness that somehow I doubt Martha would have had the deftness to deliver. It took the stillness of Mary to give me the clearheadedness to discern right from wrong, good advice from bad. And it took the perspectives only midlife can offer to keep from pandering pat answers to complicated problems.

But most of all it took trusting that God was perfectly happy with me if I just sat at His feet and listened; a belief system that, frankly, I never had the time, or the gumption, to exercise much in my younger years. And that's the magic of meno. Its hormonally driven pulsations often cause us to think outside the box of life to see the possibilities of doing things in a different way, with a certain "Mary-ness" that the drivenness of youth roars right over.

As a result I've continued to strive for that kind of stillness of soul that my youthful years powered past. I take long walks, mindfully hearing, smelling, and tasting all that life offers in those moments, without clogging my brain with to-do lists. I no longer feel guilty if I spend an afternoon reading one of my favorite authors' recent creations. (Anne Lamott, Max Lucado, and Dr. Larry Crabb's books remain some of my most soul-soothing reads. Ditto for Nick Sparks when I want pure escape.)

When I'm at my most stressed (as I was last week, when I pulled off a wedding rehearsal dinner for 50 and a wedding ceremony and supper for more than 200 just 18 hours later—both at my own home and at my own expense), I have to make conscious efforts to still my breathing and lower my tension-filled shoulders so I have no other choice than to breathe abdominally. Then I meditate, in the truest form of the word, on God's Word. When that doesn't work, a nap often does. And I'm not embarrassed to say it might take medicinal help to relax my all too often turbocharged self to pull it all off.

This stillness, this Mary-ness that I'm deeply hanging on to, often flies in the face of an American culture that frowns on calendars that aren't chock-full.

But that day I spent in my living room taught me something very dear. Something I likely could not have grasped until middle age: That stillness has immeasurable value.

I didn't earn a dime that day. I did nothing valuable enough by the world's standards to be put on any time clock or garner me any IRA contributions or vacation days. No pews at my local church would be named in my honor for what I'd done. I'd only modeled what Mary had been fearless enough to do. I sat at Jesus' feet. In stillness. In quietness that was radical enough to hear His voice. But you know what? Somehow, at the end of the day, that alone seemed like payment enough.

● ● ● ● ● ● ● ● **MENTAL-PAUSE:** ● ● ● ● ● ● ● ●

You're Either a Martha or a Mary, and Midlife's No Time for Schizophrenia

If, in your heart of hearts, you feel you've been a Martha type of person far too long and you really do want to change and believe that God will love you just as much if you simply sit at His feet, I recommend you read *Classic Christianity* by Bob George. This true classic contains a profound, life-freeing message to those of us who are repeatedly tempted to believe that we can actually earn our way into a better type of life.

And if you're so over the edge with type A busyness that you suffer from chronic muscle tension, anxiety, and overwrought breathing that makes your mind race like a gerbil running on a wheel in a cage at midnight, I suggest you think about devising your own personal Christ-centered type of meditation, relaxation, and breathing techniques to still the body and the mind. Books like Dr. Archibald Hart's *The Anxiety Cure* outline these types of exercises.

I learned the connection between my breathing and my ability to quiet my anxious insides from a Christian physical therapist some years back.

"You're not breathing, Ronna," he said as he applied counterpressure to the muscles in my concrete-tense back. And he was right. I was chronically taking tiny little breaths from the upper portion of my chest and living a life of basically uninterrupted hyperventilation. No wonder I was so Marthalike uptight!

The physical therapist reminded me that God had breathed into Adam the breath of life, and Adam then became a living soul (Genesis 2:2). With that I took probably the first abdominal breath I'd taken in years. He showed me how to put my hand on my belly and make it rise with correct diaphragmatic breathing that flooded my body, and my brain, with oxygen-infused stillness. And it has become an exercise that I still diligently practice—especially on days when I'm tempted to relapse into midlife Martha-ism.

◦ ◦ ◯ ◦ ◦

On a completely separate note, take this time now to look up the phone number of the nearest domestic violence center in your area. (Look under "domestic violence" or "YWCA" in your local phonebook.)

Give them a call to see what kinds of legal, physical, emotional, and spiritual services they offer and then carry that number in your purse. Or visit the website of the National Coalition Against Domestic Violence at www.ncadv.org. You never know when, amid your own Marymaking, you might meet a woman who desperately needs that kind of information.

Or perhaps you see that woman daily in your own bathroom mirror? Perhaps your own attempts at becoming a "Mary-ier" woman are greatly hampered by an abusive relationship. If you're not sure, go to the simple self-test at Amazon's Recovery Web (www.recovery-man.com/abusive/abusive_signs.htm). An adapted version of this self-test is provided below. And if you find yourself reflected in the self-test, get help from a counselor specifically trained in domestic abuse counseling (a specialty not all counselors, Christian or otherwise, are educated in).

If you're a Christian, ask your local DV shelter if they have *On the Wings of a Dove,* a film made specifically for Christian women confronted with the painful experience of realizing they are in an abusive relationship or marriage. Specialists say these women are often the most difficult abuse victims to counsel—ironically because of their deep commitment to their faith, a faith that, in some churches, can wrongly be used to "teach" wifely submission without emphasizing the husband's responsibility to demonstrate sacrificial, servantlike, Christlike love to his wife.

Are you in an abusive relationship? Here's a self-test.

You may be in an abusive relationship if he:

- constantly keeps track of your time
- acts jealous and possessive

- uses money, anger, or lack of affection to control the relationship
- accuses you of being unfaithful or flirting
- discourages your relationships with friends and family
- prevents or discourages you from working, interacting with friends, or attending school
- constantly criticizes or belittles you
- controls all finances and forces you to account for what you spend
- humiliates you in front of others, including "jokes" at your expense
- destroys or takes your personal property or sentimental items
- has affairs
- threatens to hurt you, your children, or your pets, or threatens to use a weapon
- pushes, hits, slaps, punches, kicks, or bites you or your children.
- forces you to have sex against your will, or demands sexual acts you are uncomfortable with

Got Game?

Facing life's inevitable failures
"so what" tough.

The words hit me like a freight train.

You know how it is. You're going along in an innocent little conversation with a perfect stranger. You have no other agenda than to put out one of life's little forest fires and solve a dilemma. Then, all of a sudden, that person makes an offhanded comment that they've probably used for years to guide their own life and—BAM!—you've discovered a new way of looking at things that will color your world for years to come. Something that maybe, even if you're a middle-aged, menopausally challenged mom like me, you've never, ever thought about before.

So it was with my pre-New Year's conversation with an academic advisor at one of my son's colleges a few years back. In the midst of writing some of my own New Year's resolutions, I had taken time out to call him and discuss some of the decisions my son needed to make for the upcoming semester's class scheduling.

This is a kid who's been a success in any endeavor where he pointed his heart. Not just any high school varsity football player, he was an All-State offensive and defensive player. In the regional playoffs, when his team was slaughtered abysmally in a 54-0 loss, he was playing just as hard at the end of the game as at the beginning, oblivious to what the scoreboard read. When he broke his arm in a rival game against another high school, he refused to leave the sidelines until he knew his team had won.

The boy has heart. Enormous heart.

But academics—especially college-level ones—had been an entirely different ball game.

High school never demanded from him what college did. So he came onto college education's playing field like many young freshmen; with high hopes but not so much as a game plan. The scoreboard (his grades) took some big hits. The temptation to quit, to walk off the field, hovered like the Goodyear Blimp over his thought processes.

"You know, of course, that failure is *always* an option," said the advisor to me, as if everyone in life had heard and believed this truth. As a mother riddled with worry that any one of her kids might not find their special niche in life, the words simply weren't sinking into me, a once-obsessive overachiever.

"You've failed in life, haven't you, Ronna?" he asked me as if the question had only one possible answer.

I know this sounds naively naive, but it was honestly something I'd never, ever stopped to think about, let alone ask myself. In fact, so good was I at dodging the self-probing question that I honestly couldn't give him an answer I was sure of.

But I was now quaking with the query that, sooner or later, hits every middle-aged woman as she looks back over her life. Have I failed in this, the only life I've been given on this earth? *Where* have I failed? And, worse yet, *whom* have I failed?

"Well…uhhh…I suppose so…" was my feeble reply. I don't know why, but my midlife memory was still glossing over the little and even the big failures in my life. It was definitely time for me to get real.

"See, everyone fails at certain times in their lives. So failure *is* an option," continued the advisor.

Fat chance, I grumbled to myself in my mind. I was not comfortable with where this conversation was going.

"Failure is ALWAYS an option. Quitting is not," he continued, not at all bothered by my painful silence. He calmly lectured me as if I were one of his own students.

By now I was wanting—very much so—to quit this conversation. But reluctantly I could feel a fiery Hot Flash from Heaven sneaking in on me like a touchdown in the last few seconds of a game.

"Listen to him, Ronna. You can learn something about My view of failure," said the voice that can speak to my heart and guide my way when my own denials don't.

I listened. Then, as quickly as I could, I politely segued my way out of the conversation and hung up the phone with both the advisor's voice *and* the still, small whoosh of that Hot Flash hanging in the silence of my office.

Is failure really an option? I asked myself. What a radically simple thought. I'd never permitted myself this kind of self-accepting talk before. Like a lot of adults my age, I'd been chased by the mental process that failure is *never* an option.

Bestselling author Anne Lamott recently wrote that she was in her mid-30s when she finally realized that a B+ was a perfectly acceptable grade. I was stunned at the thought. Here I was, well over my late forties, and still striving for straight A's.

In doing so, I had been—many times over—terrified to try. To risk. To get in the game. Or stay in the game. None of my friends who'd watched my high-energy endeavors over the years would have guessed the truth: That fear of failure had been on my life's scoreboard most of my 50-ish years. I had never thought of failure as an option—an option that wouldn't kill me if it came upon me. And so, understandably, that premise had carried over to my offspring.

That's not to say I *hadn't* failed or they hadn't failed. I mean, who on earth would be pompous enough to even think that, right? But like a crazed runner on a railroad track, I'd never truly taken time to glance back at the train that was bearing down on me, one whose cargo was a multitude of failures both large and small. And I realized that running from them was getting me nowhere fast. Nor was it setting the right example for my kids.

I was truly shaken. I looked at the list of New Year's resolutions before me on my desk and realized how safely shallow they were: Love my husband and children even more. Reach out to the poor and homeless. Let my life be a blessing to those who know me. Yada, yada, yada.

Then, in my head, I pictured the others. The ones I'd been afraid to write down for fear of failure.

Finish writing a book called *Hot Flashes from Heaven*. (Imagine that!) Start a column for a daily paper where I could at long last freely write words I felt others needed to hear. Go after a solidly established literary agent and publisher. Quit giving my personal confidence away by worrying. Trust my gut. Fear not. Try. Risk. Stay in the game.

I was nearly shaking with the ramifications. Failure is *always* an option? An option that won't be an embarrassing skeleton that needs to be stashed in yet another closet of my life? An option that won't haunt my kids the rest of their lives?

All of a sudden, in one lightning bolt of understanding, I got it. I got God's drift when it comes to how He looks at failure. If I believe His Word, then I must accept that, like that favorite Scripture of mine in Jeremiah, He has plans for me. And if those plans include a little trial, a little failure, or a little falling on my face so I can look into His as I let Him pull me up, who am I to question?

Immediately the word "failure" lost much of its power over me. So what if I fail? So what if my kids fail? So what if my husband fails? So what? So what? So what?

The only thing that gives failure any power over us at all is the often paralyzing thought of quitting that it often evokes.

My son, the one who spawned the conversation that spawned the Hotflash in my head, walked in. I could see the dejection in his body language as he glanced over the college's paperwork on my desk. The frustration at his less than sterling grades was flashing on his scoreboard.

"You know, Son, failure's *always* an option," I said tenderly.

He jerked his head up at me as if I were speaking a foreign language as I continued.

"Failure is always an option; although, I'll admit, not a fun one. Not the one we might prefer. But not one that will kill us, either. Failure's not a sin. Don't be afraid of it. We all fail. Remember the football game when you broke your arm? You couldn't play. But you stayed on the sidelines. I couldn't drag you to the ER. Your heart was still in the game. Failure is always an option, but quitting is not."

My words, like the advisor's, brought release to my son and relief flooded his body. I saw tension drain from his face.

Like the college counselor, I had just given him—and myself— permission to be human: Permission to fail.

"You know, Mom, my grades really aren't *that* bad. Each quarter they're getting better. Ten years from now I know I'd regret it if I quit school now," he said, a hopeful smile creeping across his face.

I smiled back at him. I looked down at my New Year's resolutions and started to pencil in the ones I'd been afraid to write. If my kid could stay in the game, I might as well jump in there with him. And if I fail, so what? So what? So what!

● ● ● ● ● ● ● **MENTAL-PAUSE:** ● ● ● ● ● ● ●

Being Willing to Fail Creates a Win-Win Game Plan

This particular Hot Flash from Heaven was divinely appointed déjà-vu, if there is such a thing.

After writing it, it became part of a series of Hot Flashes that appeared in a column by the same name for a local daily newspaper.

The fact that you're reading this book is another proof of the freedom that removing the fear of failure from life can win a person. After the column ran a short course, the book was picked up by an adept agent (thank you, Janet Grant of Books & Such Literary Agency), who then pitched it to the publisher whose imprint now crowns this creation in your hands.

So, what game plan have you been afraid you'd fail at?

Start the way I did, by writing it down. Want to go back to college? Go. Think you or your marriage would benefit from counseling? Go (even if you have to go alone). Need a job change? Go. Have a secret wish (like learning to ride a Harley) you've always wanted to fulfill? Go.

Boldly give yourself (and your loved ones) permission to fail—maybe even miserably. Then start running your plays, one at a time, even if the opposition pushes you backward on the field.

You'll find you'll win something even greater in the long run—a message on your scoreboard that says, no matter how many losses your game stats show, you're still a player in the big leagues of life.

Oh, and another thing about this quitting business. (This is where the college counselor and I differ.) I've found there is a time to cut one's losses and take a step back to reassess the game plan.

That same son eventually did just that. A few semesters later and still less than inspired by the scholastics that college required, he opted out for a while and began building custom homes for a living, something he's brilliant at.

His younger brother, with more than enough brain power to be a scholastic superstar, took a similar tack when the same decisions entered his life. Rather than finish college (he already had two years under his belt), he opted to buy a fixer-upper at the tender age of 19 and then put his efforts into remodeling it.

At 21, much to the chagrin of both his parents, in addition to a lucrative day job that keeps him more financially independent than many of his peers, he joined a motorcycle stunt team. And he thrives on learning—and then performing—motorcycle skills in front of cheering fans. Is that failure? Is that quitting?

Plain and simple, I really don't have the right to think I know the answers to those questions. They're not even mine to ask.

All I know is that these boys-turning-into-men are still "in the game," albeit different ones than either they or I had pictured.

They'd both boldly say they were playing life their way. And if I DID dare to insinuate that what they're pouring their entire hearts into is failure, I'm sure they'd be the first ones to get in my face and answer me back with an empowered, "So what!"

And you know what? I'd say that makes them winners I'm unbelievably proud of.

15

Come On, Baby, Light My Fire

The importance of meno-mentors when in the dark about aging.

● ● ● ● ● ● ● ● **POWER SURGES** ● ● ● ● ● ● ●

Remember, we all stumble, every one of us.
That's why it's a comfort to go hand in hand.

EMILY KIMBROUGH

Teach the older women...then they
can train the younger women.

TITUS 2:3-4

I've already mentioned that I live in the country. Way, way, deep in the country. Our little ranch lies at the base of a beautiful North Idaho mountain whose purple spire seems to hook nearly every wash-clothlike cloud that floats innocently by. Then, with the passion of a hysterical scrub lady, Mica Peak wrings every drop of moisture out of that cloud, no matter what the season. In her torrential temper tantrums, the mountain deposits the wet stuff in buckets, or shovelfuls, as the case may be, on the roads that lead me home.

So it was that late February night when I was fighting my way back from town through blizzardlike conditions. The moisture was coming at me, whipped along by gale-force winds, parallel to the ground, in the form of little white bullets of both ice and snow. The weather had crept up on me like a stalking cougar. And I was finally being forced to see (pardon the pun) that my midlife night vision had begun to dim.

In the preceding years, headlights from oncoming cars had slowly begun to look more like drunken fireflies doing the Texas Two-Step into my lane of traffic. More than once the little buggers had caused me to swerve into places on the road that I had no business being. Combine this slowly growing midlife visual disability with a storm like this one and, well, it was the perfect storm for a personal catastrophe.

It was nearing 10 p.m. by the time I knew I was in trouble.

As I made the turn off the highway, I looked at the ominous stretch of seven miles of whitened rural roadway that lay ahead of me. There were probably four inches of snow blanketing the frozen pavement, so it was impossible to see where the asphalt ended and the expanses of fields and meadows that cradle it began. It was an official whiteout, and my middle-aged eyes were completely stumped by the optical illusions it was creating.

"God, I need some major help here," I cried out as it appeared there wasn't even a track in the snow I could follow.

No sooner had I made that cry but, seemingly from out of nowhere, a vehicle's headlights instantly appeared behind me. And not just any vehicle. I could tell, even in my rearview mirror, that the broad shadow behind the lights meant it was likely a large pickup.

This was a big deal to me. You see, that meant that I could be reasonably sure that I basically had the ultimate pull-Ronna-out-of-any-ditch, snow-eating, four-wheel-drive machine now following me.

Where that truck came from, I have no idea. But I sure knew who was responsible.

"He will light your way," I heard the Hot Flash from Heaven drift down like a single snowflake in my mind.

"Gee, thanks," I said as I relaxed back into my driver's seat and even turned up my radio's tunes to sing a bit. I smiled to myself as I again looked in my rearview mirror at the four-wheel-drive guardian angel behind me.

As I turned my attention to the road in front, I noticed another surprise. With the added illumination of the truck's headlights shining out in front of me, I saw something I hadn't seen before. With or without lousy eyesight, I now could see faint indentations in the snow left by another driver who had, sometime earlier in the bleak night, forged a path before me. Now I knew exactly where to drive to keep my car on the road. The pickup was indeed lighting my way.

Suddenly though, as I crested over a hill, I saw something that the truck behind me couldn't. An enormous snowdrift lay right in our lane.

If you've ever plowed unsuspectingly into a snowdrift, you know the danger of what lies directly ahead. The chassis-sucking compaction was coming at me like Jaws, the shark. Do-do-Do-do-Do-do. I immediately hit my emergency flashers to warn the pickup. I said a silent prayer and swerved erratically to the opposite, narrower, undrifted side of the road.

Quickly, I looked in my rearview mirror. My rescuer was still behind me. In fact, warned by my flashers and skidding tracks, he was driving completely out of harm's way in the clear lane.

The truck's slower pace indicated that the driver was as shaken by what had almost happened as I was. As we made our way down the remaining miles of road, a pattern developed. As I'd see the drifts coming, I'd hit my flashers, move slowly to the left and sneak on past them. The pickup, like a newly hatched duckling with its mother, followed my lights and tracks. I marveled at the irony. *I* was now the rescuer. The driver of that truck needed *me* to make his (or her) way home just as much as I needed him (or her).

It was then that I received another one of those Hot Flashes from

Heaven as I heard the voice again, *"Did you realize that you actually light each other's way?"*

"How true, how true," I answered back as I thought about all the people in my half century of living that I'd either led or followed through the storms of life. My husband. My children. My parents, siblings, and other relatives. Girlfriends of all types and ages—both Christian and non. And, yes, even perfect strangers. We'd helped each other navigate through some very dark times and scary obstacles, both large and small.

How often had I been weak and others had come along, in front or behind me or even beside me, with just the right insights, actions, or words to light up my path? How frequently had that extra radiance, sent straight from a Creator who cares about such things, exposed hidden tracks in the road that, had I not had their "light," I would have never seen? How often had I done the same for others? And why was it that this lifelong illumination seemed so much more precious on the blurry roads through menopause? So much more necessary for survival?

There'd been Dixie. I'd stumbled into one of her speaking engagements at a local church and had been enchanted by her off-the-wall humor while discussing midlife's darker topics, such as grief and loss.

She was pushing 60. I was saying goodbye to my forties and facing my fifties shaking in my boots. I desperately needed a meno-mentor who could help me find the answers to the questions that felt like Eiffel Tower-sized snowdrifts in my path.

What would the following years look like, I needed to know? Was life over for me now that body parts were drifting southward? Would I make it through the aging process with nothing more than liver spots, shar-pei-wrinkled skin, and memories of happier times? Would my husband? Would our marriage?

Dixie wove hysterically funny personal stories in with deeply serious ones. As her talk unfolded, she disclosed the tragic loss of her only son, killed in an automobile accident at the exact same time the estrogen in her body was also dying.

With a fearless bluntness, she shared her battle with periods of depression that had taunted her ever since. And yet, minutes later, she had the room doubled over in laughter with a joke about the time she'd walked through a fancy, schmancy ladies' high tea in an apricot colored suit that made her feel as though she was the hottest babe there—only to find she'd crossed the entire room with a streamer of toilet paper hanging out of her skirt's waist band and trailing her like a very bad joke.

Ironically, it was Dixie's tragedies that lit a bonfire of hope in me. Like that big truck lighting the way behind me, her anecdotes allowed me to consider that the aging process—and the losses that come with it—are survivable and sometimes even laughable. After all, she'd not only lived through the death of a child—certainly not a laughing matter to *any* mother—but she was now, depression or no depression, able to encourage others with her own personal hot flashes of insight that had given her strength during those trying years.

Then there was Elizabeth. She'd bought herself a Harley-Davidson and learned to ride it as a personal reward for making it to her seventy-fifth birthday. One solitary road trip had taken her three attempts to make it up the gale-force, wind-laden Columbia River Gorge highway from Portland, Oregon, to return to her home in Spokane, Washington (some 400 miles away). Each time the buffeting winds had forced her to return to Portland, where she was visiting friends, and then rest up to take another try the next day.

"What on earth was so important that you had to make it home?" I'd asked the retiree, who still always keeps herself impeccably made-up and coifed.

"Why, my hair and nail appointment, silly" she said as serious as if she were discussing a cabinet meeting with the president of the United States. "I absolutely *never* miss my hair and nail appointment!"

To this day, nearly a decade later, I still vividly remember the senior chutzpah that the gutsy granny unknowingly passed on to me. "Aging can have its own brand of geriatric grittiness," was the unspoken message she'd carved out in the snow-covered pathway before me. She was more than 20 years my senior, and yet it was she who fired up my attitudes about middle age and beyond.

Like the Scripture in Titus, she and Dixie and others (including my mom and aging aunt), were *my* meno-mother-figures. And I would eventually be the same to others.

Kim is a good example. She is from Korea, and she became my "nail lady" when I wandered into her shop desperately needing a manicure. This wasn't one of those budget shops where there's a conveyor belt approach to ripping and drilling a woman's nails back into submission. Kim was different. While she'd only been in the United States just eight years, her Korean husband was a successful engineer and she'd worked in upscale nail salons on New York City's Madison Fifth Avenue. Her work was all done meticulously by hand. And so it was that I let mine rest in hers that day.

Over the several years I used Kim as my manicurist, however, the exact opposite began to happen.

Kim was some ten years younger than I, and she confided to me that her body and her mind seemed to be changing. I might add that in most Asian countries there isn't even a word in their native language for "menopause." The women in those countries simply aren't plagued by the symptoms that can sometimes unravel American and European women.

Those who study these matters have deduced that it might have something to do with the fact that the Asian diet is rich in soy, a phytoestrogen, or plant-based precursor to estrogen, which helps ramp up the body's own production of the real-deal hormone. Researchers have found that when Asian women are placed on a more Western-style diet, which Kim was now on, they begin to have many of the same menopausal symptoms as their American and European counterparts.

And Kim was baffled by it. Her main support system, her mother, still lived in Korea and couldn't relate to or answer Kim's questions. Kim's mom simply didn't understand American menopause. And, because of language barriers and personal shyness, it was difficult for Kim to ask any American woman about it.

But she and I hit it off right from the start with conversations that were part broken English and part hand signals and pantomime. Over the years I saw her we formed a friendship.

As she held my hands to do the nail work, I figuratively held hers. I comforted her when she confided that intimate relations with her husband were, ahem, drying up a bit. (More about that topic in the next chapter.) I eased her mind that the anxiety she was feeling about her oldest daughter soon leaving the nest was also normal and encouraged her and her husband to begin to revive the "coupleness" that often eludes longtime parents after years of raising teens.

I was Kim's big pickup. Dixie, Elizabeth, and hordes more savvy meno-mentors I met along the way, were mine. We formed an extended family of sorts; the kind that is so missing in our culture today—the kind our fortunate foremothers had when they needed to ask their mothers, grandmothers, or elderly aunts who lived in their midst (or in the cabin just down the road), "What am I going through?" "Is this normal?" "How did you make it through this time period?"

So it was there, in the midst of that raging snowstorm, that I got my middle-aged head around the concept that independent or not, brave or not, we truly need the headlights and hand-holding of others far more than we know as we age.

My friends and family will be the first to tell you that I wasted many years stubbornly trying to always be the unrealistically strong one. I paid a price for that mentally, physically, socially, and perhaps even spiritually. Though I had gobs of friends, for the most part I was the one *they* leaned on.

But, finally, in the sweetness of this time of midlife change, I've learned that God has a better road to travel on. For you and for me. One well-lit by His light, reflected in human relationships that are built on the more equal give-and-take of our strengths and weaknesses in good times and bad.

I've found that no one need always be "the strong one." No one need always be "the rescuer." No one need always have perfect "vision" during all those whiteouts life throws at us. It just doesn't work that way. We all need a new millennial version of the extended family. Especially during perimenopause and menopause. We aging women need meno-mentors. And we're all capable of being one to someone who, on the flip side, needs us too.

As I turned safely into my driveway, the truck continued on its way into the night. I wondered if the driver had been thinking the same thoughts I had as we'd made our way toward our separate homes. I was tempted to flick my lights at the truck as a thank-you for the little gift of light given to me that night. Somehow I felt that he (or she), maybe more than most in the evening's suffocating darkness, just might understand.

● ● ● ● ● ● ● ● **MENTAL-PAUSE:** ● ● ● ● ● ● ●

Drive Down the Menopausal Highway As Though You're Not Alone—'Cause You're Not

Have you been feeling like a lone vehicle on midlife's stormy road? I'm here to tell you that you needn't be in the dark about the aging process. The menopausal years are the perfect time to accelerate efforts to connect with others in order to hold each other's hand and share each other's light.

So keep your eyes open for potential meno-mentors along the way, older women who've already gone where you're going. Women who've done it with style and stamina, dignity and perhaps a dab of divaness. Women whose light you can use to navigate the upcoming years.

And don't overlook your biological extended families: older, female relatives who carry DNA similar to your own. Research shows that women often follow their own mother's timeline as to when they, not only start their first period, but finish their last.

Another thing it has proven is that, if your mother had a difficult time transitioning into The Pause, you might also face bigger challenges "changing." (Another data tidbit: Women who suffered from

PMS are much more likely to have difficulty handling the symptoms of perimenopause and menopause.)

So seek out those aging aunts, female cousins, grandmothers, and mothers and ask them how they handled "The Big M." My guess is that they'll be flattered that you have come to them for advice and information about how menopause and the midlife years affected them.

At the same time don't be surprised if you soon find yourself in their shoes—mentoring a younger woman into middle age. When you meet that younger woman who is now walking where you once walked (and trust me, you will), make time to help her journey in the bright spots where your headlights shine strongest.

I believe it's what God wants of us—to build weather-resistant relationships with others, and, in the process, with Him.

And don't forget the two national organizations devoted to fostering meno-mentoring-type relationships, The Red Hat Society (www.redhatsociety.com) and the up-and-coming, even edgier, Blue Thong Society (www.bluethongsociety.com).

You'll find that we aging women each have outstretched hands quite capable of latching onto someone else's. And we each carry with us a certain degree of light and vision in this important half-point in life.

Who are you to decide that yours isn't the exact radiance that someone else might need to illuminate these midlife years—and vice versa?

16

Is There a Thong Under That Muumuu, Mama?

Or...Where has all the libido gone? (Sung to: "Where Have All the Flowers Gone?")

● ● ● ● ● ● ● **POWER SURGES** ● ● ● ● ● ● ●

Passion, though a bad regulator, is a powerful spring.

RALPH WALDO EMERSON

Before a girl's turn came to go in to King Xerxes, she had to complete twelve months of beauty treatments prescribed for the women, six months with oil of myrrh and six with perfumes and cosmetics.

ESTHER 2:12

The front porch swing creaked out a rhythmic melody as it went back and forth, to and fro. It was a song I'd learned to love over the years as I often gently pumped it into a relaxing lullaby to life. I'd listened to the rusty singing of that swing for almost ten years, and it had often been the background music by which my husband and I had watched our children play, grow, mature, leave the nest, and eventually marry.

And now, with all of them gone, it still served us well as a quiet retreat at the end of the day. The swing had become a place to share a glass of wine, watch the wild ducks and geese land in the pond in front of our house, and quietly observe does and fawns grazing.

It was there that we did the things that couples do on porch swings—dream, plan, problem solve, reminisce, rejoice, and, sometimes, when life had really bogged us down, reconnect.

The swing was also a place for solitary sitting and equally solitary thoughts.

Just as often as Bill and I had sat together on that swing, we'd each spent time on it alone. Sometimes doing our own personal problem solving…or praying…or simply pondering the depressive or wildly delightful things of life on planet Earth.

That's where I was that late afternoon. Sitting alone on the swing. Hoping its hypnotizing sound and sway would comfort me in an area of my life that desperately needed reassurance.

My husband, seeing me alone on it and intuitively reading my body language that all was not fine with me, sidled over and sat down.

That action temporarily stopped the rhythmic noise of the swing. And that troubled me. It was so-o-o the metaphor I did NOT want to contemplate.

"What's wrong, hon?" my husband quizzed bravely, knowing that that's often a loaded question for a menopausal woman swinging forlornly in the fading sunlight.

I gave the porch floor a push with my feet and got the swing making that lonesome squeaking noise again.

"Do you hear that?" I asked.

"What?"

"The noise of the swing, the way it keeps perfect time, kind of like a clock ticking."

"Well, yeahhhhh," my husband answered slowly and cautiously.

I'm sure he now knew this was not going to be the simple "I can fix it for ya, baby" conversation he had hoped for.

I scooted over closer on the swing to my big guy and put my head on his shoulder and my hand in his. I never in my entire life suspected I would ever, ever, ever say the words I was about to say to him. But he was the only person in the world to whom they would matter, and I needed to tell him.

"Well," I continued, "that ticking noise of this swing is kind of like my, uh, libido."

He looked at me quizzically.

"You know, as in sex drive? And *you* know, better than anyone, that it's always been there. In raging proportions. Dependable as clockwork. Reliable as the rising of the sun. As regular as the ticking of this swing." I paused to let him hear the "click, click, click" of the swing going back and forth, then added, "And it's carried us a long, long way."

He smiled. So far, he liked the topic.

And he also knew we'd both benefited from my uninhibited embracing of my inner "wild woman" in the passion department of our relationship. It was an aspect of our relationship that had been a reliable, unrelenting, romance-enhancing constant.

Until recently.

And I was having a hard time explaining it to my bewildered husband.

"I just don't feel the same inside," I confided.

When he looked at me, I could see he thought I was referring to something physical. But I wasn't, actually. Well, maybe I was. I really couldn't tell. It was as though the switch between my brain and my body had been abruptly turned off.

"Do you mean you're not attracted to me anymore?" I could sense the concern and confusion in his question.

"No, no. It's not that at all," I replied, realizing that even that response was not quite accurate. But how do you tell your spouse of double-digit years that the passion that fueled the "engine" feels as if it's rapidly running dry, right along with the estrogen that used to ignite it?

One can't use the metaphoric word "dry" in this kind of conversation without realizing it's a more-than-apt description of the problem diminished libido brings to the marital table during the change of life.

I continued, desperately trying to put words to my dilemma which was really now *our* dilemma; because anytime a spouse's libido crashes, it impacts both parties in the marital relationship. I knew the data. Intimacy is the oil, so to speak, that lubricates the grinding gears of marital complacency. The thing that refuels a couple's love, communication, feelings of safety, and connectedness. Like noted sex psychologist David Schnarch wrote for Psychology Today's online e-zine, "Sex can be more than just a euphemism for 'making love.' It can be the actual process of increasing love, of sharing it, of whetting your appetite for it, and of celebrating life on its own terms." The lack thereof can dry up far more aspects of a marriage than just the physical. And menopause is rife with this quandary that has the potential to undermine even the strongest relationships.

"Something inside of *me* is changing," I tried to explain. "And while it's physical, it's also very mental, and I'm pretty sure it has something to do with menopause and the declining hormones that help fuel the sex drive in a woman. I just need more, uh, *time* to, uh, turn over the engine, I guess you could call it. And I need your help in doing so."

My husband still wasn't getting it completely. Even though I was talking motors, this one wasn't the kind he was used to working on. Those others he definitely knew how to fix. A new spark plug here, a rebuilt alternator there, and abracadabra, a working engine! But I was talking "girl-speak" and, unfortunately, I didn't know "guy-speak" for what I was trying to get across to him other than bungling bluntness.

"Read...my...lips," I wanted to scream at the poor guy. "Translation? More stimulation, blast it! There's a reason God gave men hands, buster, and they ain't just for fixin' greasy automobile parts! Picture l-o-n-g-e-r stimulation, buckwheat! And while you're at it, picture patience. And preparation. Lots of it. Start with that bed I make for you every morning. Thank me for it. Give me eye contact. Make it sound like you *really* mean it. Fix *me my* first cup of morning coffee. Follow *that* up with some sexy and flirtatious affection and innuendo throughout the day. You know, the kind of stuff a *young* husband automatically does with his even *younger* wife whose crankshaft he really, really wants to turnover! If you want something at night, start workin' on it in the mornin', Jack!"

But I didn't say any of those things. Frankly, I think I was a tad afraid to be so transparent and desperate and vulnerable and downright bratty with a guy I really could have trusted. I didn't want to hurt him as this definitely wasn't his fault. Instead, I gave him the calmer, more textbook explanation.

"This is totally normal, Bill. Women at this time of life just need a little more time building up to intimacy," I said as I tried to reassure not only him, but myself, that we'd get through this. And, to be honest, at the time, I'm not quite sure either one of us was really buying it.

"It'll come back," I secretly reasoned to myself. "It *has* to come back. It's so much *me*. I can't have just *lost it*. A reasonable person doesn't just 'lose' something as personal and important as this topic of conversation. Do they?"

Cold hard fact of peri- and menopause: Often they do. Or at the very least, that's how it feels.

And after a few more months of things—how do I put this?— petering out even more, we both realized that, in order to keep sexual intimacy (and the psychological marital intimacy it cultivates) a viable part of our lives, we would have to make some changes.

We would have to work at something that had once been as natural, easy, and fun as rocking on our porch swing. And, obviously, because this complication was, at the time, mainly in *my* body and *my* mind, I was the one who was going to have to dig the deepest to unearth ways around this often unavoidable part of The Change of Life.

So, I decided to go to the right place. To my girlfriend's office.

Her business cards read "Gyne-goddess." And with good reason. The sharp as a tack, certified nurse practitioner doesn't "do" obstetrics. Her focus is strictly gynecological, and thus she's specialized in her field of knowledge. She hears complaints like mine—of midlife lost libido—on a daily basis and, at the time, she could, with lightning speed, diagnose and prescribe myriad medicinal "solutions" to most any woman's problem. And that she did for me. From an effective, over-the-counter lubricating product called Slippery Stuff (that you can order over the Internet from sites as mundane as Amazon.com) to prescription hormonal creams, patches, and the like that can sometimes reboot the crashing hard drive of libido. I gave a few of them a try, but before I tell you what did and didn't work for me, I need to add something here.

Notice that I used the words "*at the time*" when describing what "The Gyne-goddess" was then prescribing. That's because "at the time" she was still a romantically robust babe in her mid-forties. Not too much later she and I would meet at what had evolved into an informal, at home, every-other-week-or-so gal-pal get-together of tea and crumpet-type delicacies as we usually discussed things "outside" the gynecological world she works in. Things like new wall colors we had picked out for our houses, new flowers we had discovered that grow well in our climate—that kind of thing. Safe, girlfriend-type things.

But this time it was her turn to divulge to me that, all of a sudden, as if out of the clear blue sky, and despite a hysterectomy years earlier, she was experiencing that dreaded loss of libido herself. Fancy that.

"I can't believe it," she said with that delightfully wry smile of hers that could turn even a routine pap test into a female bonding experience of comedic proportions. "Here I am ladling all this advice out to women, as if what they're going through is normal and no big deal, and now, BAM, it's happening to me and I don't know what the heck to do with all this. This doesn't feel normal, even though I know it is. And it is a very big deal, 'cause I'm supposed to be in the libido biz and my own engine is stuck on idle." We both laughed at her nakedly humorous honesty and the profound changes we were now *both* going through.

But she was discovering what I'd found out before her. That, while lessening libido is normal during The Change of Life (even for women who've had hysterectomies where the ovaries have been left intact), it definitely doesn't *feel* like it. As a result, it plays havoc with the few things left in a menopausal woman's life that still are normal. (Women who do lose their ovaries in a hysterectomy are instantly catapulted into menopause, no matter what their age. Those women are usually prescribed hormone replacement therapy to help them cope. Some 600,000 American women a year undergo both kinds of hysterectomies.)

I might add that I've been told that some menopausal women's libido actually *ramps up* during The Change. But I've met only one woman who admits to it, and as a result, I'd recommend *she* write her own book. I'd be the first to buy it. So would the Gyne-goddess, as we're both now officially shoulder to shoulder with our own aging, and now fragile, femininity.

And so it came time for the Gyne-goddess and me to debrief. To talk more about what goes on inside the brain—rather than the body—of the nearly libidoless midlife woman.

Yes, I said *nearly* libidoless. Because I've found out something about this libido business.

With or without a husband with the patience of Job (which mine had as we figured out what worked and didn't work in the physical department), with or without medications, lubricants, etc., it's *in there* somewhere. That desire's still inside me. Inside you. It really is. Even if, like many women, you've maybe *never* much felt it, midlife *can* be the time to finally unearth it. But, as you may have already guessed, midlife libido morphs into more of a mind-over-meno-matter.

As a girlfriend I've known for nearly 40 years recently said, "You just need to work it. All the time. All day long."

Before you jump to conclusions, let me explain what she meant by that advice. Glenna has a job. She has kids, grandkids, hobbies, a lovely home, a lovely yard, and lovely friends. (Me, of course, being one of them.) You know, all the things that have absolutely *nothing* to do with libido except to perhaps distract it even more. But she also has a husband. And a marriage. And she knows that, without that, some of the other things might not mean nearly as much to her.

So somewhere along this potholed driveway into the garage of geriatrics, she made a decision. She was going to "work it." And by that she meant that she was not giving up her sexuality without a major fight. Simultaneously the Gyne-goddess and I made similar decisions. The nurse practitioner slapped on a hormonal patch. Due to possible hereditary breast cancer concerns, I opted to follow my other friend's tracks.

"I really do have to think about it all the time, all day long," Glenna once again reiterated to me recently as she described the psychological exercises she regularly uses to keep herself sexually sharp. Now, she wasn't talking anything pornographic here. What she meant was she simply couldn't trust her body's autopilot mode anymore to get her "in the mood." So she made the decision that she and her mind were taking over the controls.

For her, that meant "use it or lose it." That term describes the medically documented, physiological chain reaction of aging sexuality. The more often you do "it," the more often you "want to." Physicians state that more frequent "senior sex" keeps a woman's inner tissues from even further drying, thinning, and literally atrophying, not to mention the age-defying, antidepressant effect it has on the psyche of both males and females. Researchers at Queens University in Belfast, Ireland, discovered that having sex three or more times a week may reduce the chance of heart attack or stroke by 50 percent! Yeah, baby! Forget the Lipitor. Let's just hop in bed and take a tumble.

So in order to beef up her efforts at "using it or losing it," Glenna found herself spending more time, effort, and even money on things that make her feel beautiful, sexy and, would you believe this? Hot. And I am not talking hot flashes hot, honey.

My friend's strategy, which I too have adopted, reminds me of a far younger woman many centuries ago who discovered the same thing about her own sexuality.

Her name was Esther. And, believe it or not, she's actually the heroine in a book of the Bible appropriately named, duhhh, Esther.

Now Esther was no winter chicken. She wasn't even a fall chicken like most of us meno-chicks. But, as a grade-A "spring chicken vestal virgin sort," she had a remarkably similar challenge ahead of her with regard to her "motor maintenance." She was a lovely young woman scheduled to meet a very powerful king shopping for a new wife. (I think his old one, Queen Vashti, was probably a prime example of menopause-gone-mad as she'd smart-mouthed the king one too many times and, as a result, had gotten the boot out of the castle.)

But before Esther had her dream date with King Xerxes, she had another date with another man: The king's "purveyor of women," Hegai.

It was his responsibility to prepare a selection of beautiful young women for their first "job interview" with the king during a time period in history when it was not considered immoral for a king to sexually "test-drive" each new prospective bride.

Want to know how Hegai prepared the women? (Smart guy, this Hegai.) He might have been a man, but maybe that made him even more of an authority on how to get women "in the mood." And bear in mind, these were younger women in the prime of their sexuality.

He gave them a year.

"A year?" I can hear you ranting. "Are you crazy, Ronna? My marriage is strained from week to week by my 'engine failures,' and now you want me to tell my husband, 'Uh, sorry, honey. I'm having a year-long headache'?"

No. No. Triple no. Because that kind of effort entails far more psychological foreplay, for lack of better words, than any woman or man our age has the energy for.

Esther's story, for those of us in these…um… "hot flash" years, is an allegory, okay? And I think we can learn something from it. I know I did.

It came by way of one of my spicier, "yeah, baby" Hot Flashes from Heaven and, ironically, it did involve the words "12 months." It also included other words, such as "beauty treatments," "oils," "perfumes," and "cosmetics," the same words used in the Scripture that describe the pampering Esther received before her potential one-night stand.

Here's what it basically said: *"Remember Esther of old? How long it took her to 'get ready'? An entire year. And that preparation may read to you like a physical thing, but it's really more mental than physical. The beauty rituals of women that make them feel more comely are closely tied to their sexual self-confidence. It's a God-given thing, not to be taken lightly. What winds up on or in the body starts out in the mind. And vice versa."*

Bingo. Hegai had hit on a bigger stimulator than we women often give credit to: *Self*-pampering and mental makeover magic that turns once impoverished possible princesses into bonafide queen material—no matter what the age.

I remember when I first caught a whiff of this extraordinary concept. Another sister-in-law, who can easily pay more for a single bottle of perfume than I do for my entire, extensive repertoire of cheap makeup, quoted me a little verse I'd never noticed before in the Bible, Proverbs 27:9: "Perfume and incense bring joy to the heart."

And I thought about Esther and all the "psyching up" she must have gone through as she prepared mentally and physically for a night with the most important man in her life—her king. Until this time I'd somewhat discounted the power of fragrance to turn a woman on and had been quite content with the inexpensive dime store varieties.

But then menopause hit and I decided that this ol' gal deserves something better. She deserves an "oil change." I went to a major department store and, after decades of pinching perfume pennies, allowed myself the luxury of an upscale brand of fragrance, heavy with the oil of real perfume. While I loved its seductive scent, I loved its name even more, even though it was hard for me to pronounce, Indecence (as in En-Day-Sans) by Givenchy. To me it sounded just a wee bit naughty and made me feel a bit more so with regard to my husband. I was moving in the right direction.

And then there was my "work it" girlfriend.

She was the first person who introduced me to thong underwear. At first I thought it was simply highly decorative dental floss.

"No, no, no," she reassured me. "It goes on the *other* end."

"You have GOT to be kidding!" I wanted to blow off her suggestion of moving from those safe, sensible granny panties that leave undie lines zigzagging across a meno-mama's expanding "motor housing" like multiple spark plug wires. Was she suggesting that changing into something more provocative just might reawaken my almost neutered inner wild woman?

Darn right. Okay, so those thongs didn't hide things quite so conveniently as the granny panties, but they sure made me feel a lot better about what I wasn't hiding. (If you don't believe me, go to the Blue Thong Society's website, www.bluethongsociety.com, and you'll find a whole lot of other women out there who agree with me.)

Lest you think I've completely lost my rocker, I will admit that in certain outfits, one does need some extra "camouflage." To which I fearlessly reply: Never discount the value of spandex! Oprah and I (my, don't *I* travel in good company!) both use a new-age, girdle-like-undergarment called Spanx that sucks and tucks places below your waist that you never even knew needed sucking or tucking! (PS: The king of the knockoffs, Wal-Mart, carries a similar product two-thirds cheaper than Spanx.)

Then came the most profound Hot Flash from Heaven of all. At first it sounded more like the lyrics to a risqué rap song than some rapturous revelation, *"Dried up don't mean dead, Sista."* I cringed at the wording and pictured all the things that also seemed to be drying up right along with my menstrual flow. My skin, for instance. Once plump and moist, it was beginning to feel and look more like parchment than porcelain. My hair, once lioness thick, was leaning more towards hyena hair than the mane I'd once had. Yup, dried up was an appropriate description for more than one of my body parts. But it certainly didn't mean I was dead yet, so why act, or look, like it?

Time for an engine overhaul.

The thongs started me at the bottom of my meno-makeover. Then I moved "upward and outward" with a few carefully selected spendy little bras that did more for me than any plastic surgery could have. My personal fav? One called "Very Sexy" from Victoria's Secret that beefs up body parts that have long since sunk south and moves them much farther northward.

As I got braver I steeled myself and headed into the "true inner sanctum" of the age challenged: The wardrobe closet. If I hadn't worn something in more than a year, out it went. If I put something on and it made me feel even moderately matronly, out it went, and in a major hurry. If I looked in the mirror and saw anything with the least bit of "frump factor" (as the Blue Thong Society calls it), out it went. Then I began the now never-ending hunt for clothes-with-a-kick that are age appropriate for me. (Picture Dr. Phil's wife, Robin. Her clothes are edgy but elegant, youthful but definitely something we wouldn't catch Britney Spears wearing. Although, she'd do well to follow Robin's example.)

Hey, Ronna, you've switched subjects on me, I can hear you thinking. *We were talking libido, remember? And now we're talking perfume, wardrobes, and even thongs, for heaven's sake.* Good choice of words—those last three. I think that it truly is "for heaven's sake" that we older women need to do some real soul searching on the mind-body connection to our God-given sexual spunkiness.

If Esther had to do the same thing in her early years, why should we be suddenly off the hook, simply because we've gotten a little "long in the tooth," a little "sag in the bag"?

I remember a very revealing trip I took with a couple dozen women a number of years back after I'd learned these libido lessons. It was one of those trips where no one knows anything about anyone else except that they are joined together by a few commonalities. Ours were: 1) the destination—we all wanted to go to a fancy, touristy hot spring in Canada, 2) our ages—we were all middle aged and, 3) a shared value system—we all shared the same faith, but none of us shared the same churches.

I observed the women and, as I was later to find out, they were closely observing me. It wasn't necessarily critical or judgmental. It's just something women do. It's how we connect. We observe.

And we all observed the same thing: That despite our commonalities, there was something dramatically different between almost every one of them and me. It wasn't a black and white difference. It was what I now call either "The Grayness Factor" or, when I'm really annoyed with it, "The Muumuu Mentality." And I've seen it in even the sweetest of middle-aged women and in my aging, churchgoing girlfriends.

These are women who've visibly lost their spark, who've disappeared onto a blank, midlife slate of what I can only call grayness. I recognize them because I was there once—staring in my mirror and seeing my face and my once-fiery spirit and even my sexuality in shades of boring grayness and sameness. And all I wanted to do was hide under a giant muumuu, the very same types of muumuus many of these gals came packing in their suitcases as their weekend wardrobes! Seriously!

The fascinating thing to me was that the women recognized the difference in me. And there was more than one of them who came to my room to ask if she could poke around in the prolific wardrobe and makeup I'd brought. I'm again completely serious!

"We feel like we're traveling with a rock star," a number of the especially gray gals said to me after I'd made a few more wardrobe changes than any of them had ever thought of making.

I didn't discern an iota of criticism in their comments. It was more a wishful thinking sort of thing as I shared with many of them the words that I'm taking a full chapter to present to you. In fact, one of the older ones, a darling "girl" much older than me, paid me a lovely compliment when she said, "When I grow up, I want to be just like you."

By the way, when I say muumuu, you know what I mean, don't

you? I'm referring to those drab, tentlike outfits that loudly broadcast, "I have lost *it*. In fact, I don't even remember what "*it*" is I've lost, but I've surrendered to the loss, and now, you know what? I simply don't care."

That loss can be a synonym for so many important interconnected things in a woman's life that ultimately lead back to her sexuality: Her self-confidence, her self-image, her self-value, and her belief in her own outer and inner beauty.

That's why I can't write about inner things like libido without mentioning the external things. I think that's also why Hegai put such an emphasis on his girls luxuriating in a year's worth of beauty treatments to prepare to meet the king. It takes more than a little primping, powdering, plucking, and perfuming to psyche any princess up to queen quality in her mind and in her body. Why should we old broads be any different?

Then why do so many of us oldsters spend less time on it than our younger fellow females when they're the babes who need it the least, and we're the ones who need it the most? And why are so many of us in such denial about the defeminizing power a muumuulike outfit and impoverished personal pampering has over many a meno-mama's sexual mojo (mojo being another word for "charisma" or "charm")?

I know none of us dares answer all those tough questions for the entire meno-majority. We respect each other far too much for that. I think it's enough to answer these questions for our own selves.

As a result, I've decided that while Bill might be my "right-hand man" in the libido department (pun most certainly intended), it is *I* who needs to be the chief mechanic of my own "motor maintenance." I'm the only one who can make *me* into an Esther for my kingly husband. (Do not tell him I called him that. The ol' guy already knows he has got me wrapped around his little finger. No need to give him more ammunition.)

That said, does anyone have a spark plug in their makeup bag I can borrow? My husband's taking me out for a romantic dinner date tonight. I think I'll have oysters.

⚫ ⚪ ⚫ ⚪ ⚫ ⚪ ⚫ **MENTAL-PAUSE:** ⚫ ⚪ ⚫ ⚪ ⚫ ⚪ ⚫

Motor Maintenance Works Both Ways

In aging, "motor maintenance" is not necessarily gender specific. Husbands have their own challenges in this department. Just as a woman's estrogen levels decline, so too do many a man's testosterone. Thus, the frequent scenario whereby older guys who were once impatient and temperamental jerks blossom into mucho mellower males; men so mellow that their libido takes a nosedive as well.

That can be either a bane or a blessing for their libido-challenged ladies. A bane if the wife is still feeling the need for the emotional and physical connection that sexual intimacy produces but is having trouble getting her own engine to turn over. A blessing if, well, you can figure that one out for yourself.

Other things that can affect male libido are medications and/or medical problems (including potentially serious prostate problems). But the biggest reason for a decline in libido with aging men is depression (a hugely undiagnosed problem for men because, unlike women, they rarely seek out help for it).

If you think your guy could be in the gutter of male depression, here's a list of symptoms that might help him, or you, make the diagnosis and get him the help he needs.

These symptoms, by the way, are adapted from a more extensive male depression self-test in Dr. Archibald Hart's ground-breaking book *Unmasking Male Depression.*

Note that the symptoms of male depression are markedly different from those of female depression. The key ones being that whereby women become sad and teary when depressed, men become mad and irritable. Where women blame themselves for their depression, men blame others—a convenient circular emotional phenomenon that can keep both partners depressed.

Hart's book is a must-read for any woman living with a chronically grumpy husband (one of the primary symptoms of male depression) who may manifest that depression with sexual disinterest.

Depressed males:

- Become irritated easily.
- Blame others for their depression.
- Can have diminished libido.
- Act out their inner turmoil (vs. turning it inward the way women do).
- Need to maintain control at all costs.
- Are overtly hostile and aggressive.
- Try to fix the depression by problem solving.
- Turn to sports, TV, sex, alcohol, workaholism.
- Can become compulsive time keepers.
- Lose their drive and ambition (numerous job changes).
- Try to maintain a strong male image.
- Are terrified to confront their weakness.
- Are bothered by things that never used to bother them before.
- Have restless sleep and either sleep too much or sleep too little.
- Become angry, even when they don't show it.
- Have angry outbursts they can't control.
- Seem to be unhappy.
- Feel their life is a failure.
- Need "things" to make them feel better.
- Often sit around doing nothing.
- Sulk, pout, or are moody to the point that they can't help it.
- Have a difficult time achieving intimacy in marriage or other relationships.

Now back to the topic of this chapter—the aging woman's sometimes fading libido.

Here is a caveat I simply can't dismiss. If you're a happy-as-a-lark, gracefully graying muumuu mama and you and your husband both love it, if you can truly say that your contentment is not simply resigned complacency, and if it doesn't interfere, whatsoever, with your self-image and you or your hubby's joy in your marriage and intimacy with each other, then forget this entire chapter.

But please do me a favor and write a chapter of the Hot Flashes of insight you've gleaned from the heavens that have gotten you to that unique place of embracing grayness and your loss of your sexual identity. I promise I'll include portions of the best ones in any possible sequel to this book. Send it to me at jcleaveronahog@gmail.com.

The Sandwich Generation

Caring for others can melt ya faster than grilled cheese on a slow burn.

● ● ● ● ● ● ● **POWER SURGES** ● ● ● ● ● ● ●

When it is dark enough, you can see the stars.

CHARLES A. BEARD

Those who won't care for their relatives, especially those in their own household, have denied the true faith. Such people are worse than unbelievers.

1 TIMOTHY 5:8 NLT

You must be so proud of him," she said enviously.

I wanted to throw the phone down at Brenda's comment. I was talking with a girlfriend, bemoaning the fact that one of my children was, despite being grown and gone, still having some financial challenges. I told her my husband and I had begged him to move back home for a few months to build up a savings account and find his financial bearings.

He'd refused.

"You must be so proud of him." Those words, and what she meant by them, still echo in my mind today.

She didn't say them lightly, I was to find out. Her son had just moved home for the umpteenth time, making him part of what society has now coined "The Boomerang Generation." Children of baby boomers who leave the nest and then ricochet back, some even dragging their own families with them.

That can often catapult the middle-aged mother, who simply wants her life to slow down until her hormones catch up, into another unenviable group's nickname: "The Sandwich Generation."

You see, my friend was not only worrying about her boomerang children finding their niches—and their own homes—in life; she was overwrought with health concerns over her husband's widowed mother and even her husband. He'd just been diagnosed with heart problems. Her mother-in-law was showing the first signs of Alzheimer's, and Brenda was now making twice-weekly visits to her home with groceries. Brenda had become sandwiched between caring for the people she loved the most. And the warring within the "worry zone" in her heart was simply too much for her. Her marriage was paying a heavy price. And so was her health.

"It's like launching a ship," one of my husband's friends had bragged one day a number of years ago, when explaining why he'd sent his kids off to Harvard and then financed their stay well enough that they didn't have to get jobs while they were there.

"You do everything you can to make sure the ship's ready for the voyage, and then you release the anchor and let it go," he'd explained, barely hiding his feeling of superiority over what he felt was a well-thought-out plan. His words had left my husband questioning his requirement that our kids have some kind of job while they went to college and that they each invest a little of their own money in their own education—even though they all knew we'd saved enough for each of the four to go to college, with or without their own financial assistance.

Some eight years later, all three of the man's children have moved back home with him with those pricey college educations and without grown-up professions. "Boomerang" is right. That same father is sheepishly stymied by what to do with the three of them to get them out of the mud they're mired in. On top of that, he's sandwiched with caring for a cancer-ridden wife. The guy's melting down faster than grilled cheese on a slow burn.

The boomerangs are oblivious. They know they have a lifeboat docked at home. It has a well-stocked galley and enough gas to go the distance. That leaves them with enough disposable income to buy the necessities of life, like Prada handbags and jet boats. (I kid you not. One of our friends' boomerangs recently tried to pull that aquatic purchase off. Fortunately, that was the last straw for Mom and Dad. They gave him six weeks to move out and stuck to their guns.)

Years ago I would have been horrified at the thought. I'd always known that my own mother would have opened her doors to me anytime I'd needed her. And therefore I felt the same way about my own kids.

The key was, once I'd pulled up anchor, I'd never returned to the harbor. In fact, the thought had never even been on my sonar once I was gone. Even when my house burned down, it never occurred to me to move back in with my mother. And I don't know a fellow boomer who did.

But I do know vast numbers who now have those boomerang kids. And many of these midlifers, especially the X chromosomed ones, are now feeling the added squeeze of the aging parent or ill spouse who also needs their help. That kind of pressure leaves them pressed like a vise grip between the loves of their lives without much time or energy for their own. As a result, they, and often their marriages, are running on empty.

Sandy was one of them. Her often-derelict son, the one she'd sacrificed thousands of dollar for by having him educated in a private Christian school, boomeranged back more often than he'd gotten "F's" on his former report cards. Unfortunately, she'd found his bouncing back home a blessing full of irony. At least then she knew where he was. When he wasn't crashing at her house, he had a nasty habit of spending the night on a jailhouse bunk.

At the same time her elderly mother was getting more and more ill and demanding more and more of Sandy's care. She was the only sibling left in her mother's hometown. If Sandy didn't do it, who would? Her husband wasn't likely to step up to the plate. He had a hard enough time simply making it to the low-paying job he held. Sandy was the major breadwinner in the household. And did I mention she had breast cancer? The girl's "grilled cheese" was blackened by the heat of more stress than one woman should handle.

Then one day a strange thing happened. For some inexplicable reason, Sandy's grown kids and husband came home to find all of their belongings they'd failed to pick up in their house strewn, cyclonelike, across their very visible front yard. Boxers in the begonias, Levi's in the lilacs. You get the picture.

Inside, Sandy was contentedly munching on a grilled cheese sandwich. Whoops, sorry, I made that last sentence up. But she might as well have been. She'd been sandwiched to the max, and she'd had it.

That's the downside of the sandwich generation. And, frankly, that's what I expected this entire chapter to be about. But I did another one of my scientific surveys. (That would be by way of quizzing random older female strangers at a women's Bible conference I attended.) And their answers, in many ways, surprised me.

Yes, they'd been through the sandwich years, they admitted to me. And even before it was called that. This phenomenon is not new, these older women assured me. Adult parents have always been sandwiched between the love and obligation for their own parents and their offspring.

These gals may have been beyond boomer age, but they were still young enough to remember the times when they had aging parents—and grown children—who sometimes needed them. But what surprised me most was their perspective, one that's been recently reflected in numerous national news specials done on the topic of "sandwiching." Its name? "Acceptance."

Now, first I need to add a disclaimer here. I am not yet, per se, grilled cheese. But with our only remaining living parent a mother who's now heading toward her eighties (albeit living wonderfully independent with largely excellent health in her mind and body) and four grown children each finding, and making, their way in adult life, I have to admit to occasional bouts of feeling sandwiched by concern. I am also not yet a caregiver, the term given to anyone who is having the cheese squeezed out of them by hands-on duty. But despite that, I still feel inclined to give out copious amounts of care, sometimes spreading myself, and my worry meter, far too thin.

NBC reporter Rehema Ellis recently reported the latest PEW (an independent public opinion research group) study that cited that 13 percent of people 41 to 59 are in true crisis mode, caring for aging parents at the same time they are caring for growing kids; or, more stressful yet, the kids of their kids.

The women I talked with had been there and done that. And they had that thing that only getting past a trying time can give: perspective. The kind that yields acceptance. And an attitude that more than one news program exploring the sandwich generation's dilemmas espoused along with my informal quiz group of women; one I found surprising: family first.

We all know what that means. It's the opposite of the "me first" attitude many boomers grew up with in the '60s and still often tout today while whining about the responsibilities of being sandwiched. But my informal group of women exemplified it best when they described the years spent sharing their homes with either their elderly parents or their grown children and their children's children—or a combination of all three. They admitted that it was, indeed, stressful. And challenging.

But looking back on those years during some of their darkest family times, they now see the stars. They see the positive in the night sky of their challenges. They see the family relationships that were enhanced because of and not in spite of the trials they went through. They see the good that came out of it; the multi-generational closeness it fostered, the patience it encouraged, the forgiveness it taught. At a stage of life when it would have been highly tempting to hang on to their "me first" attitudes, they chose the high road; a road outlined in the Bible's 1 Timothy 5:8, "Those who won't care for their relatives, especially those in their own household, have denied the true faith. Such people are worse than unbelievers." That choice, they would add, was not without ground rules and expectations.

The women all stressed that they didn't open their homes carte blanche (like the examples I gave at the beginning of this chapter) to freeloaders, no matter how much they loved them. There's a difference between loving care and enabling. And it's far too easy to slip into the enabling mode. But the loving mode—and the Scripture that encourages it—was something they simply couldn't turn their back on.

And so it was with them as they entered and lived in—some for several years or more—sandwich relationships with their next of kin. Some drew up rules. Others contracts. Others simply prayed. And prayed. And prayed.

In doing so they watched their young adult married children save up precious money for their first down payment on a house—and appreciate it. They observed their mothers passing on the love and wisdom of their generation to not only their grandchildren, but sometimes their great-grandchildren as well. They came to know their parents, and their children, and sometimes their children's children, in a whole new way. And vice versa.

"This is the way it used to be," one former sandwich confessed to me, "when families were clans and lived just down the dirt road from each other's cabins or farms; before there were warehouses, like rest homes, to care for the aged. Before families were so frequently separated by long distances and self-absorbed lives."

The sandwich didn't know it then, but her words became a Hot Flash from Heaven quicker than it takes cheese to melt in a microwave. God didn't need to say it directly. As He often does, He used a human to convey His message.

And I was staggered by the ramifications.

The reasons these women's perspectives are so different from the ones I opened this chapter with is that they all, without exception, accepted the fact that life is filled with sandwiching responsibilities and the stress they can create. They also emphasized that their family first attitude had to extend into their own marriages as well. They confessed that they had to guard their primary marital relationship at all cost to make the others work. And they also all admitted that sharing their home with returning family members did create strain on their marriages and the way they and their husbands interacted.

What helped a lot was their unspoken "eleventh commandment": "Thou shalt not enable freeloaders." That went for kids and aging parents alike. The kids were required to have viable savings accounts and jobs that contributed to the end goal of them having a nest egg with which to hatch their own family lives. Elderly parents were given ways in which to contribute that were age and ability appropriate, even if it was only folding the family clothes. "All members must stay productive" was the grease with which they coated the cheese sandwich grill.

For some of them, the time did eventually come when tough decisions inevitably needed to be made. Parents' health needs sometimes became too taxing for many of the sandwiched to handle and the parents oftentimes *did* need to be moved to extended care facilities—often in the face of tears and even a few angry, guilt-inducing accusations from the elderly. (Those accusations eventually softened with time.) Children and grandchildren alike needed to learn specific "rules of engagement" with regard to respecting the home and possessions their parents had worked all their lives for. And they needed to stay on course toward building lives of their own.

The ones who didn't encountered the Bible's version of tough love. (Second Thessalonians 3:10: "When we were with you, we gave you this rule: 'If a man will not work, he shall not eat.' ")

Did that mean they stood by and watched a loved one starve? Of course not, but it did mean that sometimes parents have to watch their kids, and sometimes their own parents, go through tough lessons in life without bailing them out.

Did all of this prevent cheese meltdowns? No.

But it's important to note that the women I talked to, the ones I hope to emulate, should I ever land in their former dilemmas, all made a conscious decision. They deliberately and prayerfully chose to step back and look at the messy stuff of being in extended families.

Then they made a choice. They chose to accept that all of the above is part of being in a family, part of what makes us human. They chose to put family first. Then these brave women deliberately and prayerfully scooped up the melted cheese of life around them and opted instead to make a macaroni and cheese casserole with it that fed their entire family tree.

● ● ● ● ● ● ● **MENTAL-PAUSE:** ● ● ● ● ● ● ●

What Goes Around Comes Around

While none of us ever wants to be in the category of "the cared for," the realities of the aging boomer demand that we give some thought to it. How will we handle it when the shoe is on the other foot? When we are the cared for instead of the caregiver?

Have you thought about what it will cost you or your loved ones if and when you need more care than they can supply? Granted, that might be 20, 30, or even 40 (God-willing) years from now. But that will only make it more expensive, not less.

And what if it's not decades from now? What if it's 20 weeks from now? Twenty days from now? A woman I know was recently diagnosed with lung cancer. She was barely five years older than I am now. She died 20 days later.

Have you made a will? Perhaps purchased long-term care insurance? (It's inexpensive if purchased when you're 40, 50, or even 60). Long-term care insurance provides in-home and/or nursing home care for the one in three people in America who will spend the on average two years of their life in such a facility. Such a stay will cost, again on-average, $70,000 a year, an expense that can quickly gobble up a person's retirement savings and assets.

While my husband and I haven't purchased nursing home insurance, we did purchase a piece of rural acreage ten years ago and designated it "our nursing home insurance." It has increased in value ten-fold so far.

As in most things in life, what goes around truly does come around. I hate to say it, but any of us midlifers are just one stroke, one heart attack, one doctor's scary diagnosis away from having the tables quickly flipped on us.

That's really important to remember. The Bible's entire "do unto others" philosophy holds true even in the aging process—maybe especially in the aging process. As a result, I find myself more magnanimous with my mother as I see myself facing the same issues I might have previously preached to her, "Buck up, Mom." And the same holds true for my kids. I see the bigger picture now, and I find that my words go much further when they're oftentimes not said.

The five words I do frequently use with my kids—those four kids who've refused to return to the nest no matter how much it might have helped them—are the ones my friend originally said to me. The words I once questioned. "I am SO proud of you." And I mean it with all my heart.

18

Checking Your "Re"-Tire Pressure

Making sure you've got what it takes for the long haul into retirement.

● ● ● ● ● ● ● ● **POWER SURGES** ● ● ● ● ● ● ● ●

Life begins at retirement.

AUTHOR UNKNOWN

*Ants are creatures of little strength,
yet they store up their food in the summer.*

PROVERBS 30:25

I looked up at my husband's image through the motor home's massive front window. He was sitting in what we'd soon call "the pilot's seat," warming up the engine. I was outside, loading the final vestiges of our supplies to last us several months down south. Where's "down south"? Neither of us had any idea. All we knew was that we were dipping our toes into the waters of retirement and hoping neither one of us would get too burned.

Shoot, I thought to myself. *He looks like one of those old geezers you see tooling down the highway in their mansion on wheels that they barely know how to keep on the road. The kind I get so ticked off driving behind.*

Gulp. That meant that as soon as I climbed into the copilot's seat I just might not look so young and hip anymore, either.

Such are the quandaries of the retired.

Or the almost retired.

See, we hadn't quite taken "the big step" yet.

It's a scary one, this plunge into the world of retirement, and not one to be made lightly. And so we were moving the way we'd always done life. Slowly, cautiously, and conservatively. We bought a relatively inexpensive, nice, but older first-step motor home, one we could easily sell if we decided the lifestyle wasn't for us. We knew we didn't want a second home. We had already had one and knew all it did was burden us with more responsibility and more stuff, not less. And that's what we, like every other retiree we now know, wanted. Less, not more, stuff.

I was taking my computer and I'd still be writing. Bill would keep our contracting company's heavy equipment, knowing he could always go back into business in the spring when we returned, if retirement proved too hard of "work" for us. There were lots of unknowns and only one thing we knew for sure: We were headed where there was sunshine and bare ground without snow.

Snow. The first thing we learned on that maiden voyage into retirement was the startling revelation that "winter is optional." Thus the term "snowbirds." And, at least for this year, that's what we were going to be.

And while I'm using the word "optional," we would—in the years to follow—learn that retirement holds more of those things called options than many of us know. But I'm jumping ahead.

Like our peer group, we'd looked forward to this time period nearly all our lives. And here we were on the cusp of it. That snowy day we drove out of the driveway with our Harleys in the trailer behind us and pointed the nose of the RV south was both terrifying and tantalizing.

It was terrifying because we were headed into more than a few unknowns—the greatest of which was whether or not we could actually afford to take this step. Whether or not we were "cut out" for this retirement business, financially and psychologically. Could we make the numbers work? Had we saved enough? And could we step down from a lifetime of work and being responsible, all the while staying pleasantly busy and fulfilled?

I also knew this little trial retirement we were embarking on would necessitate leaving behind a network of friends and a growing family that now included a brand-new grandson who would be six months old by the time we returned. I would miss those first precious months of his life, and the thought was chafing at me like a wet diaper.

At the same time this trip into the unknown felt tantalizing because, well, it was a trip into the unknown.

I cried most of the way down there.

"Down there" turned out to be Scottsdale, Arizona—not a bad place to divert a girl's longing for hearth and home; what with all the trendy shopping and eateries, immaculate architecture and landscaping, palm trees and seductive sunshine. We found a lovely new RV park nestled in the gorgeously scenic desert on the outskirts of the city, pulled into a space, and turned the motor off. For nearly three months.

I quit crying.

So mesmerized was I by the saguaro cactus, russet-colored rocks, and rose-drenched sunsets that the nearly hypnotic hold of my "old" life lost much of its talonlike grip on me—and my husband.

While I still continued to pray for our grown kids, the distance away from them served me and them well. I could no longer "check in" on their lives. It was too far for me to run to their rescue. Phone calls home focused, for the most part, on the positive. Parental-anxiety drained out of me. My kids loved it. I was finally out of their hair. Our marriage thrived on the "we time" of being alone together on a strange new adventure.

"I am where you are," was the Hot Flash from Heaven that sustained me through long walks on the desert alone or with my husband.

As RV life took on a routine of its own (with me getting up before sunrise to write; my husband, for the first time in his working life, having the luxury of sleeping in day after day), I felt the reassurance that God had not forgotten me simply because I was living life differently. I hadn't slipped off His radar screen. There could still be meaning and purpose in my breaths—even if I temporarily breathed them in a 350 square foot tin can on wheels.

After my husband and I worked out the inevitable bugs of RV life (like my repeated insistence that he fold his bath towel in thirds so it wouldn't dampen the toilet paper it hung next to and squabbling over whose precious closet space was whose), we settled into a depth of relationship not known within the framework of a 4500 square foot home. And we found we liked it. We also found it led us to dig deep into the financial concerns that often hold people back from taking the big jump into permanent retirement.

By thinking outside the box—something getting away fosters—we were able to make brave and bold decisions about assets. Which to keep. Which to liquidate to give us more physical and financial freedom. As we tried on a postretirement budget, living as though we were no longer working for a living, we found that we didn't spend much less than when we were working. Surprise, surprise.

So we began unloading more of our stuff. We sold our business to our son and our vacation home to a developer. At the same time we checked off more weeks on the calendar that we planned to spend "snowbirding."

We liked the fact that, in many ways, we'd become turtles, taking our home with us in a slower and more relaxed lifestyle. While it was sometimes an annoying negative, it was also a relationship-enhancing positive that neither of us could escape the other for very long. There was nowhere to run to. No civic meetings to attend. No customers or clients demanding our time. If we had a fight, our close proximity to one another demanded we settle it quickly. Same with financial bickering.

"Gee," said one girlfriend back home, "I guess you'd really have to like your spouse to live the way you're living now."

That was another Hot Flash from Heaven moment for me, a feeling of "arrival." Of realizing that we did actually not only love each other but like each other too. And it was doubly compounded by the tin can experience. Of being thrown into the kind of closeness that comes from knowing no one else in a city. And being forced to make new friends quickly, friends we both liked. Having the luxury of time on our hands, we looked for other couples in the same position, dabblers in retirement just like us.

RV parks are crammed full of them.

Granted, at 52 and 57 we were relatively young for both the RV experience *and* retirement. And it was a trick to find couples as "young" as we. But hauling our Harleys with us helped. We easily connected with other younger biker-snowbirds who were also newly exploring the options of retirement. And we discovered that we were joining a rapidly growing group.

The average age of retirement in 1910 was 74; the average age in 2008 is nearing 60. Retirees are joining the ranks at younger and younger ages. That said, retirement, per se, is a fairly recent concept. Before 1935, when the federal government initiated Social Security, people usually only quit working when their health or body demanded it.

While I now love retirement (whatever that means for a home-maker), I'm not sure our society, as a whole, is better off. Although work is work, it can be rewarding and fulfilling and give even the most purposeless person a sense of purpose, a reason for getting up each morning, which could explain the all-too-common anomaly of the man who dies shortly after he retires. And it is an adjustment for male and female alike.

In contrast, retirement can be the day of playing hooky that never ends, something akin to never-ending nirvana. The golden years plated in 24-carat gold life and leisure for those of us who make the decision to spend them well.

And that, I can say with experience, takes serious planning. So we spent much of our RV time that first year with our new fellow retiree wanna-be's crunching numbers, discussing budgets, and analyzing the issues that one faces when first thinking about forever quitting working.

"How much is enough?" would be the common question we all wanted answers to. Experts agree that most retirees need at least 80 percent of their current income to retire. And that doesn't allow for an average annual 3 percent inflation rate, meaning your money has to grow to keep up with inflation, in addition to yielding you that precious 80 percent of your preretirement income each month.

The more we talked with others in our age bracket, the more we realized that many in our peer group who are still stuck working their day jobs may wind up with some seriously flat financial tires on the road to retirement.

"So how much do you think you're going to need to retire?" I dared to ask one 43-year-old girlfriend recently. Unmarried (and without a spouse's retirement income), she'd made enough employment changes that she'd never accumulated much of an IRA. And she wasn't much of a saver, either.

"Uh, maybe $100,000," she answered back, obviously just throwing a figure out.

"Okay, so let's do the math," I replied knowing that at 43 years of age accumulating even $100,000 sounded like a monumental task. "How much do you need to live on each month?"

She needed nearly $4000 a month for living expenses and to pay off her house and debt load.

"What kind of a yield do you think $100,000 will give you over a year's time?" I again quizzed.

She, who had never consulted with a financial expert, felt it could yield ten percent. Since my husband and I meet with a stockbroker several times a year, I knew that she *might* possibly find a mutual fund that produced that kind of yield.

"But you need to deduct three percent simply for the growth of the economy," I explained. "That leaves you with seven percent. Seven percent is $7000 a year to live on *if* you have $100,000 in a good solid, safe mutual fund that actually yields on average ten percent. And there are no guarantees."

Silence echoed on the other end of the phone. And I'm afraid a similar silence is ringing throughout our land as baby boomer after baby boomer has a serious caucus with their calculators, savings accounts, and visions for retirement.

Those of us who sat around those many RV campfire rings that winter on the Arizona desert were sobered by the thought of what our generation faces. But it needn't be so scary, says recent Oprah show guest Jean Chatzky, author of *Make Money, Not Excuses*.

Chatzky maintains that people, especially women, need to quit hiding behind excuses and get with the program with regard to making retirement plans—no matter what their age. "Plans," of course, being the optimal word. It's never too late to start making them and then thinking ahead, claims the reformed spender who is now editor-at-large for *Money Magazine*.

She recommends serial spenders make like the scriptural ants who store up for the winter in a take-no-hostages approach to budgeting that can take future retirees out of the red and into the black.

For some of us, financial issues will be greatly simplified if we've got a company-provided or government pension that kicks out a guaranteed X number of dollars and medical benefits each month. But less than one-third of Americans will fall into that category. For the rest of us, like my formerly self-employed husband and me, numbers we in our early thirties might have dismissed as superfluous—like the cost of taxes and all kinds of insurance (car, home, health) and their rapidly escalating price tags—will have a serious impact on our nest eggs.

Some will find that downsizing may reduce financial *and* responsibility loads enough to free them up to retire comfortably. Some will likely pick up a part-time job in one season to help facilitate travel or recreation in another. Still more may find that they can combine work with pleasure in the form of "fun jobs" or "retired occupations," such as traveling nurses (deliberately transient nurses who move from town to town as the need, or whim, propels them), or working campers, individuals who work at the campgrounds, RV parks, or condos they winter or summer in.

But since nearly half of all Americans have nothing saved for retirement, there will be a whole lot of "others." Unless they turn to experts like Chatzky and do a makeover on their spending and saving habits, the only retirement "net" they'll have to fall into will be the Social Security they have been paying into all these years. In most cases it pays out only about 40 percent of what a person regularly makes—a far cry from that 80 percent analysts recommend for those golden years. And so many of them will, by necessity, keep working to one degree or another.

In some ways, my mother fell into that category.

But I learned something from studying her as she still works two part-time jobs for extra spending money in her late-seventies. She could afford to quit altogether, but an unrelenting work ethic drives her. And this, it turns out, is a good thing.

As a result, her mind has stayed sharp as a tack, and she is still a robust contributor to society because of her decision to not retire completely. Surprisingly, while my husband and our fellow retirees have opted to do less of it, working does have important social, mental, and financial upsides to it—even in retirement years. Maybe especially in those years.

Whether or not we work out of option or obligation, it's important for all of us to remember that *"He is where we are."* No matter what stage of life we're in. No matter what our bottom line reads.

Regardless of how one segues into those retirement years, there are inevitable challenges, especially for those whose identity has long been their occupation.

Women seem to have an easier time of it than men because, over the previous years, they have most likely invested in friendships, social groups, volunteer work, helping out with grandchildren, and home and garden puttering. Many men, on the other hand, in their inherent maleness, sometimes come up lacking in those areas and have to dig a little deeper to rediscover interests that give them a sense of connection with life and others.

I found it amusing on that first trip south that my husband, who'd long dreamed of retirement, had me immediately print up business cards for him that boldly proclaimed his occupation as a "Leisure Specialist." And even now the confirmed retiree still maintains two hobby jobs in security and law enforcement work that bring him a feeling of accomplishment and belonging that he does purely for the sheer enjoyment of them—on his terms, setting his own hours, his own seasons that he works, etc.

I've had more than one phone call from girlfriends whose husbands wandered forlornly around the house for months while trying to find their bearings in retirement.

"His job may have changed dramatically," more than one of them complained. "But mine is still the same. When do *I* get to retire from *him?*" Some even got part-time jobs just to get away from *him* and the unending rat race of "homemakerhood."

One girlfriend, upon experiencing The Change of Life and her husband's retirement simultaneously, stunned the man she'd cooked breakfast for nearly every day of his adult life.

"Cook your own breakfast," she said respectfully but assertively, one day. "I'm retired too." Bingo. You go, girl.

And you know what? The next morning he did. I must say, the ol' geezer's become surprisingly adept in the kitchen. You go, guy.

● ● ● ● ● ● ●   **MENTAL-PAUSE:**   ● ● ● ● ● ●

On Your Mark, Get Set, Go!

If you haven't sat down to figure out a retirement plan, preferring instead to take the ostrich approach, now's the time to pull your head out of the sand and do so.

Start by listing and tallying all your expenses. Put that amount in one column on a piece of paper. Second, list your assets and their realistic value upon liquidation in another column. Third, write down your total debt load. Be aware that the equity in your home, while liquid, is still not entirely disposable. You will always need a place to live. And that is always going to cost money.

Then do the simple math. Subtract the third column from the second one and compare it to the total in the first. What you have left is what you have to work with today. And today is the day to get yourself on the road to a livable retirement.

First, call friends who appear to be more fiscally wise than you. These are likely people who are largely debt free and have planned for their retirement carefully. They should also be people who live in the economic strata you do. Ask them who their financial advisor is, where they put their money to make it grow the most prudently and safely, and what advice they would give to someone planning their retirement.

Then get a referral to their financial planner and set up a meeting. (Financial planners such as stockbrokers do not charge anything for these types of consultations.) Take the figures above with you and ask them to help you devise a game plan that's realistic for your age and abilities right now.

A word of caution: Meet with more than one financial planner to get a consensus as to what the largest hurdles are going to be to your retirement. Keep in mind that most financial planners are also brokers of some kind who sell stocks, bonds, CDs, mutual funds, annuities, etc. (They make money off the commissions of the products they sell.) While these products can help expedite a speedier savings plan, you'll want to select an advisor who has your best interests at heart and is not simply selling you something so he can retire sooner!

And remember that whatever kind of prognosis you get from a financial planner regarding your retirement future, *"He is where you are."* Meaning, if you've failed to plan wisely for your future, God, in His infinite wisdom, has not. He will be where you are. Like the Bible states, He will never leave you, never forsake you (Hebrews 13:5). If He can provide food for even the ants, He can surely help you provide for yourself, no matter what your age is.

19

Eternal Dove Bars

The bittersweetness of accepting death and loss.

● ● ● ● ● ● ● ●   **POWER SURGES**   ● ● ● ● ● ● ● ●

God pours life into death and death into
life without a drop being spilled.

AUTHOR UNKNOWN

There is a time for everything, and a season for every activity
under heaven: a time to be born and a time to die…a time to
weep and a time to laugh, a time to mourn and a time to dance.

ECCLESIASTES 3:1-2,4

heard him howl in a way I've never, in all the years we've been married, heard my husband cry out.

I was in my upstairs office writing. He was downstairs in his. And yet the howl rang through our home like the death dirge of a lone wolf. Though our offices are on opposite ends—and on opposite floors—of our large home, his words wailed out with perfect clarity.

"It's just not fair," I heard him repeat several times before breaking down into strangling sobs.

I ran to his office doorway. "What on earth is wrong, Bill?" I asked almost hysterically. It had to be bad to bring tears to my husband's eyes.

"It's just not fair," he again repeated, this time more angry and desperate than the first, as he stared at his computer screen with tears streaming down his cheeks.

I ran to his desk and encircled him with my arms as, over his shoulder, I read the e-mail that had brought him to this. It was from a friend of ours from many years ago. Dottie was a tall, slender blonde in her forties who, despite having had three sons, still kept her model-like figure and a toothpaste commercial smile that could light up the stained glass windows of even the darkest of churches.

I read the beginning words. "My beloved Davey Bob..." She was the only person in the world I know of who called her gorilla-built husband with a lamb's heart "My Davey Bob." To all the rest of the man's hundreds of friends, he'd always been just "Dave." A gentle giant with a heart even bigger than his biceps.

They were a perfect match, those two, right from the start. We'd known them at the very beginning of their romance. Dave had lived with us for a short time when we were newly married and he was a bachelor trying to figure out a new direction for his life.

In his early twenties he'd just made a profound decision to walk away from his old life of hard-core street drugs and aimless living and into the brand-new and cleansing waters of baptism and God's forgiveness. And walk away he did. He threw the syringes in the trash and never again, for the rest of his life, looked back. He and the woman he would eventually marry were addicted to only two things: Loving God and loving anyone else who was privileged to get to know them.

For the next 20 years or so they continued on with a life of joy and peace that made even fellow Christians sometimes sit up and take notice. And though they lived in another city across the state, we occasionally kept in touch. A Christmas card here. An e-mail there. That kind of thing.

It was in one of those e-mails that we'd first received the news several years before when Dottie would write us to say that doctors had discovered an odd-looking spot on "My Davey Bob's liver." "Would we pray for him?" she asked.

"Of course. Done deal," we e-mailed back. Dave was young. He was virile, full of life, and in otherwise good health—at least we all thought so at the time—and loaded with infectiously happy, deep-down-in-the-gut faith. The kind of extreme faith that would go out on any precariously flimsy limb to embrace a miracle from God.

Eventually that is where he and Dottie and their three sons wound up. On the very tip of a wind-racked limb of faith made fragile by the unrelenting onslaught of illness. That innocuous-looking liver spot eventually got labeled with the fearsome "C" word. Cancer.

Surely there's been some mistake, we originally thought. *God will move on behalf of this guileless, God-loving family man. The spot will disappear. Dave will give God all the credit for his healing and he'll inspire hundreds because of it.*

And much of that did happen. Except for one thing. The spot did *not* disappear. In fact, others joined it and, as a result, the e-mail prayer request updates became more frequent.

We read as one intrusive medical test led to another, one bright hope to another dashed one. But we never expected that final e-mail that brought both the tears and the agonized questions of God my husband and I made as a result of it. Dottie's "My Davey Bob" had peacefully slipped out of our world and into the next.

My husband looked at me through a goulash of grief, shock, and fury. And then he began to argue with me as if he were arguing with God. And, in a way, he was. "Why Dave? Why such a beautiful young family in the prime of their lives? Why such a great YOUNG guy? Why? Why? Why?"

I wrestled with his questions because, while they might have been about a friend across the state, we both instinctually knew that it was about more than that. It was about the unflinching fact that aging forces us to face: That none of us—none of our friends or our loved ones—will ever leave earth without first passing through the bewildering birth canal of death. And, as a result, it virtually guarantees that every person will eventually experience soul-wrenching, faith-testing, gut-level grief and loss and those horrible "why" questions.

Eventually I trudged back up the steps to my office and also howled at God, "It's not fair!"

The Hot Flash from Heaven that answered me was immediate, sure, strong, steadfast, and lengthier than I would have ever expected. And it has changed how I, and my husband, now view death—even inexplicable ones—ever since.

It went something like this, and it started with some amazing questions: *"What if you were standing in line on a 110-degree summer day, in the sweltering sun, waiting to get into an air-conditioned ice-cream stand where you'd receive the creamiest, sweetest ice-cream bar you've ever had in your life? What if you'd been in that line a long, long time and I, God, seemingly arbitrarily picked one of you out of the line and moved that person to the front of the line? What if that person was younger than you? More innocent than you? Nicer than you? Would you say that was fair?"*

"Well, sure," I replied. That made sense. I couldn't picture myself getting mad at that scenario. I'm pretty patient at waiting in line. What's a few more minutes or days? What's a few more years or decades?

"So, Ronna," I heard that Hot Flash rumble like a healthy heartbeat, *"What DO you REALLY believe?"*

That question had eternity written all over it.

"Do you believe that there really is a time to live and a time to die? Do you believe that there REALLY IS a heaven? That it could be earth's equivalent of a Cappuccino Chocolate Thrill Dove Bar for those who get to taste of it? How GOOD do you REALLY think this life on earth is when compared to eternity? Could it be that, as good as this life can sometimes be, it's nothing really more than standing in line on a 110-degree day when compared to what waits in store for those who love Me?"

By then I knew where this metaphoric questioning was leading me. I had another one of those grown-up decisions that grown-up issues force us to make. A decision we all eventually have to make about life.

And death. And eternity. And God. And even illustrative Dove Bars. And I asked myself, what do I REALLY believe?

The pat answer is, "Sure, Lord. I believe." But that's not so easy to say when a dynamic young Christian family man has been moved from the warm embrace of believing in miracles to the cold, sanitized silence of a morgue. Nevertheless, that's what I tentatively replied. "Lord, I DO believe—despite the fact that none of this makes sense to me. Help my unbelief."

The reply was as soft as a person's last breath on earth.

"Think of it this way. If there really IS a heaven waiting for you, Daughter—and only you can decide that by where you place your faith and what you do with it—then all of this will ultimately make complete sense to you someday as to why I move certain sweet souls to the head of the line. It may not be until the other side of eternity that you truly understand, but be assured that these actions are definitely not arbitrary. And, no matter how they look in your eyes, they're not punishment either—for the ones I move forward in line or for those I choose to keep behind for a time. Moving to the front of the line IS a reward. Not a reward that's visible in this life, but a reward that's crystal clear in the reality of an eternal ice-cream stand on the other side of death. Standing "in line" in life is not the reward, even though people are often duped into thinking it is. Do you get THAT?"

I had to admit that I did. It was, after all, the only plausible explanation that could give me—or anyone else—peace at a time like this. I nodded. It really did make perfect sense.

"Oh, and by the way," the voice trailed on, *"Just in case you doubt Me, trust Me to work all these events together for an even greater eternal good for Dottie and My Davey Bob's sons. Even this. Especially this. I'll do things with these individuals, and this family, that I couldn't have done with their loved one on earth. And they, too, will someday understand, but maybe only when they, too, slide over into the gentler side of eternity. Trust Me. And trust Me for them when they feel too wounded and broken to trust Me for themselves."*

How could I not trust a God who called Dave "My Davey Bob"

too? The waiting-line-for-ice cream scenario makes perfect sense if a person has eternal vision. But for many of us, that's a big "if." So let's put it this way: Isn't it really the *only* thing that does make sense during a time of such grave loss?

Can any sane person truly believe that all of life and death is only random coincidence? That it's nothing more than just a big cosmic coincidence that the tide goes in and out at a precise time each day? Autumn trees to turn red and yellow in just the right season? To me, it takes more faith to have faith in *nothing* at all than it does to believe that there is Someone much greater than I in charge of my life and my death. I dearly gobbled up the taste of that kind of faith-filled perspective: The kind Dottie's "My Davey Bob" would have been the first to remind me of.

I went to our freezer on the off chance I might find a Dove Bar hidden somewhere in its recesses and I could intimately savor the flavor of this revelation that had brought enormous peace, comfort, and resolution to my sadness. No such luck.

I knew it'd take more than a trip to the local grocery store to satisfy my bittersweet tooth of sorrow.

Looks like I'll just have to get in line and wait, I thought to myself, picturing myself in the grocery store's checkout line with a box of Dove Bars, and for some strange reason that sentence made me smile. I'll bet "My Davey Bob" was smiling too.

● ● ● ● ● ● ● **MENTAL-PAUSE:** ● ● ● ● ● ● ●

Grieving Takes Time; Proceed with Caution

I know, I know, I know. You don't have to tell me. This chapter's simply too pat of an answer, too flip of an answer, for anyone in the moonless midnight of their grief. And you're totally correct. So please don't show it to someone in that situation unless you think they might be ready to read it. I'd be a callous fool, and so would you, to tell anyone freshly grieving the loss of a loved one the things I've written here.

Dottie recently outlined the things people did do that helped her through her grief. "Anytime someone tells me something about My Davey Bob or reminds me of something about him, it is like precious water to a very thirsty soul," she explained. "I cherish it. I drink it up. I think about it over and over. Those memories are so dear!"

Amazing, isn't it? That because of her grief the dear woman is probably light-years ahead of most of us on the gratitude meter. Other gestures Dotty appreciated were:

- Reminders of God's promises to her—how faithful and good He is—something she still totally believes.

- Verbal and/or written reminders of her husband that let her know people have not forgotten him or her or their children. (Needless to say, she wept when she read this chapter.)

- Trustworthy male role models who came alongside her children to remind them what "mature maleness" looks and acts like.

- Loving her through her anger at her loss, and sometimes her anger at God.

- Being a safe place for her to cry, talk, vent, and even be quiet.

- Asking her personal questions about how she is doing, what she's feeling (even when she doesn't know what she's feeling).

- Loving her and expressing that love.

- Praying for her (even when her faith might seem nonexistent).

- Social invitations that helped fill her sometimes frighteningly empty calendar.

- Respecting her right to not ask for help.

Dottie remembers little of the first year after the loss of her husband. "It was just a fog," she explains. But she does clearly remember some of the more stupid and most painful things people said to her during that time period:

- That the person knows how the widow feels when they'd never lost a spouse. ("I just wanted to pop them one," says the spunky widow.)

- That they were just checking in on her at the one-year mark because they'd read that a person returns to "normal" by then. (She's never spoken to that person since because, in some ways, her life will never be the kind of normal she still, years later, desperately misses.)

- That "one of these days" she will know why all of this happened. (Which is clearly different than this chapter's message—that we may never know WHY until we, too, are on the other side of eternity.)

The still-beautiful blonde has made peace with that. And now her primary goal is to live a life that honors both her heavenly Father and the earthly father of her sons. I think it's working.

She relays a story of when one of her older sons took his hard-earned savings to have an expensive artist paint a picture of him and his dad. "I finally asked Jordan, 'Was your daddy your hero?' And, his response was 'I want to be just like him.' "

She divulged, "Another burst of tears came. That evening I will cherish forever. That is what I am seeing in all three of my boys. Their care of me is incredible—they will one day be incredible daddies, incredible husbands. It's just part of their makeup—created by our Lord—with an example set by My Davey Bob."

To which I've got to admit, I'll raise a Dove Bar in salute to heaven. "Davey Bob, when I get where you are, buddy, your next Capuccino Chocolate Thrill Dove Bar's on me."

20

Re-Nuptials:
The Refueling Stop

It's not how a relationship
begins that so important. It's
how it does or doesn't end.

Love seems the swiftest but it is the slowest of all growths.
No man or woman really knows what perfect love is until
they have been married a quarter of a century.

MARK TWAIN

What therefore God hath joined together,
let not man put asunder.

MARK 10:9 KJV

O ur four grown kids' orders were strict.
    "Beat it. Leave town. Get a room. Whatever. For 24 hours."
And so, there Bill and I sat, the day before our thirtieth wedding
anniversary. We were on the banks of Idaho's Coeur d' Alene River,
seated at a picnic table in front of a new motor home we'd bought
the day before. It's one of those posh mini-condos-on-wheels with

four slides, cherrywood cabinetry, and more flat screen TVs than Costco—an appropriately grand gift to ourselves to commemorate the passing of three decades together.

Over a bottle of red wine we toasted the greatest fruit of those 30 years of combined turmoil and triumph, pain and passion: our daughter and three sons, ages 21 to 29; their various mates; and our new grandson, all of whom we adored, and who we suspected were either painting our fading cedar home or perhaps, at the very best, inviting a few friends in for a modest anniversary celebration.

The former was what we were betting on. Our home needed sprucing desperately and the kids knew what a daunting job it would be for two old goats like ourselves. The latter, we deemed, was a long shot. Our kids, after all, were busy with their own lives—usually to the point of not even remembering that this date in May was an annual reminder that they were some of the rare kids in their peer groups whose parents were still actually married to each other.

We also tipped the glass to a well-timed phone call from my literary agent, surreally received via cell phone on that same remote riverbank, informing me she'd just sold my first book, *Hot Flashes from Heaven*, to Harvest House Publishers. No matter what was happening back at home, the weekend was already magical.

It was about to become even more so.

My husband leaned over the table and looked me in the eyes with the same look that had stolen my heart more than three decades ago.

"So...knowing all the good, the bad, and the ugly," he said, and then he paused shyly. "Would you do it all over again? If you could turn back the clock, knowing what you know now, would you *still* have said yes?"

I knew all that question implied. We both knew we'd had a less than stellar beginning.

"We're getting married on Friday," my husband-to-be had said nonchalantly that Sunday in 1976 as we were dodging traffic and jaywalking, hand in hand, across First Street in downtown Spokane,

Washington. "Bring your clothes and come." As if that weren't romantic enough, he added the tantalizing capper to his, ahem, proposal. "Oh, and if you want to, pick up a box of donuts on the way."

That should have served notice that my life with this man would probably not read like a Danielle Steel romance novel. The fact that I didn't hear from him for the next five days should have lit up any caution lights I might have had on the dashboard of my decision-making process. But it didn't. I was 25 and crazy in love with this man of few words.

And so I arrived at a pastor-friend's house, five days later, hoping Bill hadn't forgotten the day. I was wearing a new T-shirt I'd bought on sale (hey, it had lace on it, and it was ivory!) and a multicolored woven, also marked-down, skirt. My dowry was a box of freshly baked donuts. In less time than it took to make his proposal, we said a quick vow that included really only one word that Bill and I remembered over all the years to follow, "Commitment."

It was that word that resonated in me as I pondered my husband's question.

I doubt that any couple, in 30 years of marriage, doesn't at least once consider throwing in the towel on that word.

But the most important thing remained: Neither of us had ever done so at exactly the same time. Neither of us had, as the Bible calls it, ever fully decided to "put asunder" the promise we'd made to each other. I remembered the words of an elderly man much wiser than me when asked by a reporter what the secret was to his 60 years of marriage to the same woman. "Well," he said, smiling mischievously, "I guess neither of us ever fell out of love at precisely the same time." Ditto for us.

The Amplified Bible puts it this way in Ecclesiastes 4:9-10,12: "Two are better than one, because they have a good [more satisfying] reward for their labor; for if they fall, the one will lift up his fellow. But woe to him who is alone when he falls and has not another to lift him up...And though a man might prevail against him who is alone, two will withstand him. A threefold cord is not quickly broken."

Over the years we'd come to realize the wisdom and strength in looking at marriage as a cord of three strands.

We'd each helped the other up. Many, many times. When I'd been tempted to jump ship, it was Bill who'd cajole me back up the gangplank. When Bill had been tempted to hole up in a proverbial cave of man-land, I'd lure him out. When it seemed as though conflicts and stresses threatened everything we were desperately hanging on to, when both of us were precariously near falling, that third strand—a commitment to a God we took enormously seriously—held firm. Without it, and Him, our rope would have surely unraveled.

I stared back into his searching hazel eyes. My own teared up. "Yes," I replied. "Yes, I'd do it all over again."

Little did we know how prophetic that interchange would be.

The next morning we arrived at our oldest son's rural home, just down the road from our own ranch, at the exact time our kids had instructed.

One after another they all marched into our motor home. Like Bill said as he watched them walking single file to our RV, "All our little ducklings lined up in a row." I smiled at the sight of our progeny and their mates who were now the legacy of that cord of three strands. As I did, I said a silent prayer that someday, they, too, would be celebrating their own decades-long milestones of marriage to the same person.

They sat us down on the coach's sofa. Our daughter, Libby, a commercial banker from Medford, Oregon, handed me an envelope addressed to her father and me. *Scratch the idea that our house has just been painted,* I chuckled to myself, as I opened a lavishly layered invitation decorated with my trademark color and vehicle, a purple Harley-Davidson. *Must be a party.*

"The Snyder children joyfully invite you to join them…" I started reading aloud and then I sucked in a deep breath of air. I couldn't see the rest of the words—they were hidden behind a secondary piece of cardstock that warned, "Shhhhhh, don't say a word. Mom and Dad will not know about the celebration until that day."

I looked up at my kids questioningly. This invitation looked far too formal for a simple party. It looked...well, it looked like a wedding invitation!

Could it possibly be, I thought to myself? I didn't dare hope. *No way,* I reasoned. No way could they know. No way would they care that perhaps one of my deepest regrets in my marriage was that we hadn't started it with a ceremony that was more befitting what would be a lifetime commitment to the word "commitment."

No way could they understand how embarrassed I was of that stupid little skirt and T-shirt so many years ago, that blasted box of donuts. Over the years I'd tried to hide it from my kids and focus on the fact that it's not how a marriage begins that's important. It's how it does or doesn't end. It's whether or not one or both of the couple ever decides to "put asunder" what God has surely joined together.

What can I say? Kids pick up on more than we parents give them credit for.

I continued reading aloud. "...to witness the second wedding of their parents."

Oprah calls it the ugly cry. You know the kind. The one where your eyes, nose, and face get all red and puffy and there's nothing pretty about it? I was there. In the full-blown ugly cry. My husband's eyes were going there too.

Our kids had little time for sympathy. They were on a mission— and a deadline. The invitation said the wedding would start in less than six hours. "Dad, you go with the guys," ordered my take-charge daughter.

I bawled even more. I knew what that *had* to mean—that I would finally get to see my handsome husband in a tuxedo on his wedding day.

"Mom, you're going with the girls." The ugly cry morphed into slobbery sobs. This could only mean one thing. A dress. A wedding dress. Finally a *real* wedding dress for me.

I had no idea there would be so much more, that the "re-nuptials," as we would come to call them, would be a refueling stop for one of the sweetest, most confirming Hot Flashes from Heaven I would ever receive.

But back to my beautifully bossy daughter. It turned out that Libby had had her own wedding gown cleaned and it was waiting, with appropriate jewelry, veil, tiara, long gloves, shoes, and even a purple garter, at my mother's house in the Spokane Valley. I'd remembered buying that dress for my daughter's wedding just four years before. At the time I'd vicariously thought it the most beautiful dress in the world and promised myself there would be nothing close to a T-shirt and skirt and a box of donuts for *my* baby girl on her big day.

The dress fit me as perfectly as Cinderella's slipper.

As my own daughter lovingly adjusted my veil, I looked in my mother's mirror. An ugly cry more powerful than the White House Rose Garden's entire sprinkler system erupted.

We returned to the motor home that was now parked behind our barn, where I couldn't see anything that was going on down at my house. Libby put the final touches on my hair and makeup, trying to repair the damage caused by multiple ugly cries, and then she mysteriously disappeared down to the house.

At promptly 6:30 p.m. my oldest son, Justus, loaded me, in full bridal attire, into the sparkling clean bucket of a brand new $300,000 tractor (borrowed from a local dealer-friend). He handed me a massive bouquet, the stems wrapped in purple ribbon. Below us at the house I could hear the music, "She Thinks My Tractor's Sexy," start up. It was a song I knew my farmer-ly husband would chuckle over.

After 30 years my pumpkin has finally turned into a carriage, I thought to myself, grinning like a Cheshire cat as we rolled down the driveway, my five-foot train drifting gently in the breeze from the bucket of the tractor.

As we rounded the corner to my yard, I glimpsed wedding-central for the first time. In less than 24 hours my children (and a slew of loved ones) had pulled off the whole shebang: dance floor, DJ, photographer, white lights everywhere, tables with white linens, a huge buffet dinner, chairs lining the bridal aisle, a hundred or more guests (my daughter had stolen our e-mail and address books), wedding archway, pastor, seven groomsmen and seven bridesmaids (two of whom I'd served as bridesmaid in their own weddings some 36 years ago!), my grandson as ring bearer; and, most important, the groom-to-die-for, my husband, looking more handsome than I ever remember, in a tuxedo.

Dang, he cleans up good! I thought to myself as I caught sight of him. My brother walked me down the aisle in my deceased daddy's stead as I desperately bit my lip to prevent another ugly cry from getting the best of my makeup and gown. It didn't help that as my hubby and I locked eyes, he was ugly crying too.

My girlfriend Kathi Jingling, women's pastor at Spokane's Life Center Church, headed up the "I-do-re-do." She spoke eloquently about what this passage of time represents in this day and age, and what it means to those of us in midlife who've stuck it out with the same spouse in that three-strand cord of hope. But it was my oldest son, Justus, who brought the audience to tears as Kathi handed him the microphone.

Justus is a cowboy. The real deal. He graduated from the University of Idaho on a rodeo scholarship. He team ropes on several circuits—even won a world-championship saddle at the National Finals Rodeo in Las Vegas a couple years back. A lariat hangs in his diesel pickup as regularly as air fresheners hang in city boys' Beamers. And he embodies the archaic slogan "Real cowboys don't cry."

But when he took the microphone, his brimming eyes and rosy nose told me he now embraced the fact that "Real men do." With his other two brothers, Shiloh and Simeon, standing beside him, he emotionally and passionately spoke to the audience about the value of a person's word. How it seems so out of vogue in our culture today. "But 30 years ago," he continued, "my parents gave their word to each other. They made a commitment and stuck to it."

Through my own tears, I smiled at the thought of all the temptations Bill and I had dodged to keep that word. And how now, in retrospect, our children had truly appreciated that three-strand cord they'd so often seemed oblivious to.

With my gloved arm wrapped around my husband's, we surveyed the reward: Our children lined up as bridesmaids and groomsmen, our yard overflowing with loving well-wishers. As we listened to our son thank us for never giving up, a Hot Flash from Heaven drifted into my thoughts as delicately as the doves our children released into the air when Kathi next proclaimed to my husband, "You may now kiss the bride."

Minutes later I would share it with the crowd as my husband and I prepared to cut into our glamorous three-tiered, purple-embellished wedding cake. Beside the cake one of our guests, who'd known the story of our paltry beginnings, had artfully arranged a three-tiered pile of freshly baked donuts.

I reached for a nearby microphone.

"Many of you don't know *why* our children chose to surprise us with this lavish ceremony," I said as I described that wedding-on-the-fly so long ago. The crowd chuckled when they heard the donut part of the story, but then they grew somber as I shared with them the Hot Flash of insight I'd just received.

"A question came to me in the recesses of my soul," I explained. "You can call it from God, or just my vivid imagination, but I swear I heard a voice ask me gently, *'So, Ronna, if you could have had the perfect wedding 30 years ago or this blessed surprise, with all your grown children gathered around you to revel in it with you, what would you pick?'* "

"I didn't have to think twice about my answer," I said as I looked into the glowing faces of our friends and family. "No doubt about it, Lord. I'd have picked this." I waved my hand over all our children had pulled off in less than 24 hours.

With that, I opted not to feed my groom that traditional first slice of cake. Instead I reached for a donut and, in unison, we both bit into it together, as cameras flashed, capturing the moment forever.

I've decided, after 30 years, that I rather like donuts.

● ● ● ● ● ● ● **MENTAL-PAUSE:** ● ● ● ● ● ● ●

Life's Circular; Enjoy the Ride

Like Hot Flashes from Heaven, life at midmark is literally ripe with full circle events for those of us who keep our minds, eyes, and ears open enough to recognize them when they finally show up.

Surely, by now, you've seen a few of those in your own life. If not, look carefully. They're likely right around the next bend in your midlife road. And they should give all of us hope for the future, that God can bring full circle events that started out less than perfect and repackage them, well, perfectly.

Remember chapter 9, the story of how my first grandchild arrived in the world with an unmarried mom and dad?

As my girlfriend, Pastor Kathi Jingling, had carefully prepared her words for our unorthodox "re-wedding" ceremony, she later told me it wasn't Bill and me who were in the forefront of her thoughts. It was my son, Simeon, and the mother of our grandson, Sarah, who were.

"Nearly every word I wrote, I wrote for their ears, not yours," Kathi would later confide to me. It must have worked.

Two days after our re-nuptials, Simeon and Sarah, who were, of course, in our bridal party as a bridesmaid and groomsman, called and announced that they, too, wanted to get married. At our home. On the same lawn where we'd celebrated our anniversary. In little more than three months.

During that time period, the kids met weekly with Kathi and her husband, Ron, who gave them premarital advice and mentoring. And it was Kathi who returned to our ranch a few months later to marry the couple. My grandson, Simeon Braxton, who was nearing two years of age, was the ring bearer.

As I close this book, the "new" Mr. and Mrs. Snyder have just purchased their first home and are just days away from the delivery of our second grandchild, a granddaughter named Hannah. I find myself, once again, pregnant with anticipation at what Hot Flashes from Heaven the most assuredly gritty and grimy, but equally glorious, future will divulge as I age even more. And more. And more. Ain't it grand? I can't wait.

A Note from Ronna to You

As I close this book, another one of those Hot Flashes from Heaven hit like a spot on the *New York Times* bestsellers list. (Now THAT would be a particularly thunderous Hot Flash!)

I stare at the last few blank pages and think, that is so-o-o-o like God. To leave me... to leave you...with blank pages. *"That's what life is,"* I'll bet you can hear Him say to you the way He did to me. *"It's a series of blank pages,"* He explains. *"And if I am the Author, Daughter, YOU are the pen."*

So as you ponder this book's Hot Flashes from Heaven, what do you hear Him telling you to write on the pages of *your* life?

I'll give you the lines and the space, girlfriends. It's up to you to fill them in...

_____

_____

_____

_____

_____

_____

_____

About the Author

Ronna Snyder has been a contributing editor and regular writer for many magazines and newspapers, and she speaks at women's events. She also rides a purple Harley-Davidson and has a passion for helping women find joy and freedom by living their lives at "full throttle." She lives near Coeur d'Alene, Idaho, with her husband, Bill, and they have four children, a son-in-law, a daughter-in-law, and two beautiful grandchildren.

If you would like to contact Ronna, please visit her website at www.ronnasnyder.com.

Other Good Harvest House Reading

FANTASTIC AFTER 40!

Pam Farrel

Popular speaker and bestselling author Pam Farrel challenges and inspires the baby boomer generation of women with 40 unique ways to shape a fulfilling future, embrace God's truth, and uncover their unique purpose.

FINDING GOD'S PATH THROUGH YOUR TRIALS

Elizabeth George

Elizabeth reveals how people can "count it all joy" in hard times by understanding trials are not punishment; realizing God's grace is sufficient; and trusting Him to use everything for His plan. You are reminded that God is in control, and in Him you will find help, hope, and meaning.

GETTIN' OLD AIN'T FOR WIMPS

Karen O'Connor

With humor and wisdom, speaker and author Karen O'Connor urges fellow baby boomers to celebrate every moment. Personal and gathered stories capture the trials and joys faced when one survives and surpasses middle age.

GIRL TALK...GOD TALK

Sally Miller

The joy and comfort found between girlfriends reflects what believers can experience in their relationship with God. Through the lens of friendship, Sally reveals ways you can build an ongoing dynamic prayer conversation with Jesus.

THE POWER OF A PRAYING® WOMAN

Stormie Omartian

Bestselling author Stormie Omartian's deep knowledge of Scripture and examples from her own life provide guidance for women who seek to trust God, maintain a right heart, and give their lives over to God's purpose.